The Transportation of Transformation

From present power to purposed potential

Copyright Page

The Transportation of Transformation: From present power to purposed potential

Copyright © 2023 by Dr. Endya Perry.

All rights reserved. In accordance with the U.S. Copyright Act of 1976, this publication shall not be broadcast, rewritten, distributed, transmitted, or copied, in any form, or stored in a database or retrieval system, without prior written permission from the author.

Library of Congress Cataloging – in – Publication Data

Author: Endya Danielle Perry
Title: The Transportation of Transformation: From present power to purposed potential
Registration Number: TXu 2-396-714
Identifiers:
ISBN 979-8-9874746-4-8 (hard cover)
ISBN 979-8-9874746-3-1 (paperback)
ISBN: 979-8-9874746-5-5 (e-book)

Acknowledgements/ Dedication

I am grateful.

Anything that I ever achieve, accomplish, or complete in life is due to the grace of God. So my first word of gratitude goes to God.

Transformation has the immense power to transport people from their present power to the potential power they are purposed to reach. I can definitively make that statement because I have been blessed to travel along the journey that comes with the transportation of transformation. It is the fruitful result of this journey that motivated me to write this book. The transportation of transformation is truly a life-long process. I continue to embark on the transportation of transformation with excitement, endurance, and expectation.

This is not a journey that is taken alone. I am truly grateful for those who have and continue to support me in the transportation of transformation. My family, my friends, my corner, and my team have all contributed to my personal and professional growth, development, and transformation.

To my family: I am deeply appreciative of your unwavering support and encouragement. You freely share your wisdom and provide me with the necessary tools and qualities to overcome challenges and seize opportunities. You push me to leverage my present power. Furthermore, you also support me in my unyielding refusal to settle for my current level of success and value. I appreciate your unwavering support, understanding, and belief in me as I continue to strive for the next level of potential I am purposed to achieve.

To my leaders, mentors, and coaches: Your willingness to invest your time and energy in my development has not been in vain. Thank you for offering opportunities for me to grow, develop, and continue to transform. I will continue to employ what you have taught me to exponentially impact the lives of those I encounter. I appreciate your partnership as I continue to strive for my purposed potential.

To the readers of this book: Thank you for your attention and focus on the information, concepts, and practices presented in this book. My hope and prayer is that this book provides clarity, purpose, and guidance as you travel your personal journey of transportation through transformation. Thank you for investing in your growth and development.

Table of Contents

Introduction i

Leverage Your Present Power 1

Activate Your Motivation to Move 43

Prepare for Your Journey 101

Achieve Your Purposed Potential 151

Resources i

Introduction

There is power in movement. I am truly grateful to be in a state where I can reflect on my life and see the results, which serve as the premise of this book. I have seen what is possible through the transportation of transformation. When I think of where I come from, seeing where I am leaves me in awe. I come from a place much different from the place in which I now stand. I come from a place where I once questioned my worth and my value. I come from a place where I had someone look me directly in the eye to tell me I would never reach my goals and that I had no future. I come from a place where the statistical projection of what was possible for my life was not promising.

But the point is that I have come from that place and have now arrived at a new place. I am now abiding in a place where I realize that limitations are

Introduction

invitations that I can choose not to accept. I now stand in a place where I realize that, through faith and grace, what may have seemed impossible has been made possible. I am now in a place where I realize that I have a purpose. I also realize that I possess the power and responsibility to fulfill that purpose. The way in which I was transported from my former place to my new place was through transformation.

It was transformation that allowed me to transition from coward to courageous and from being conquered to becoming a conqueror. Transformation provided the transportation for the journey from fear to fierceness and from defeat to dominance. But it was indeed a journey. It is a journey I am continuing to travel. For the process of transformation is an ongoing, continuous process that reaps benefits along the way.

Introduction

This book is intended to be a guide for this journey. This book aims to create awareness and provide strategies to aid you in overcoming various challenges you may encounter along the way to reach the next level of your purposed potential.

You can be transported from your current state to your purposed potential for which you were created. In order to fulfill your purpose, you must transform. It is transformation that will transport you from your present to your future. It is transformation that will prepare your mind for the next phase you enter and the next level you will reach.

Transformation is defined as a process occurring within the underlying deep structure that results in a radical change in form, appearance, nature, or character. Therefore, transformation is not a slight alteration or a small adjustment. Transformation is the process of transitioning from one state

Introduction

to another. This is where the perspective of leveraging transformation as transportation is derived.

The most fundamental and catalytic belief is that transformation is possible. We all face periods of change in our lives. But what I have come to learn is that I can also initiate change within myself at any point in time. I have the power and ability to transform my thinking, and therefore I can transform my being so that I can arrive at a different destination.

As we begin this journey from present power to purposed potential, we start with identifying your present power.

1

Leverage Your Present Power

You have value. If you do not read another word in this book, if you do not gain anything else from this book, please get this: You have value. Regardless of where you come from, what you have done, or how much money you have, you have value. You have worth. You have a purpose. I am intentionally stating this in the present tense.

Right now, where you stand, you have value, worth, purpose, and power.

At times, you may feel as if your value, worth, or power have diminished. Do not allow your feelings to deceive you.

Leverage Your Present Power

Do not allow your emotions to cause you to forget what you know. You have value.

Even if others are *unable* to see it, your value exists. Even if others *choose* not to see it, your value exists. If something is not seen, it does not mean that it does not exist. Not being seen does not negate or diminish the power that is present. For example, let's say I am looking to purchase a flashlight. I go to the store, and I explore the various models of flashlights. The flashlight only becomes functional when the battery, which is in a hidden compartment, is in place. Although the battery is not visible, it is the component that provides the necessary power for the flashlight to fulfill its purpose.

It is through a battery that chemical energy is converted into electrical energy[3]. Without the battery, the electrical energy will not be realized. Some batteries are extremely large and

Leverage Your Present Power

easy to see. Others are very small and difficult to see with the naked eye. Whether the battery is easy or difficult to see, has no bearing on the importance or existence of the power inside the battery.

Another interesting point regarding the hidden power in batteries is that electrical energy is not generated unless the battery is placed appropriately. Have you ever seen a battery placed inside the correct compartment backwards? It appears it is not functional. But with one change in direction, that battery can bring light to a dark space. That battery can insert sound into silence. That battery can cause movement where there once was stillness. One change in direction can cause the power within that battery to go from being dormant to being purposeful. Many perfectly useful batteries have been thrown away simply because they were incorrectly placed and their power was overlooked or misunderstood. Sadly, there are also many people who have been thrown away or cast aside because no one saw their value. Many people have been judged by others before they were provided the opportunity to be properly positioned for success.

One of my father's favorite poems also echoes the reality that value and power exist even in situations where they are unseen and misunderstood. The poem is entitled *The Touch of the Master's Hand*, written by Myra Brooks Welch[6].

The Touch of the Master's Hand
'Twas battered and scarred, and the auctioneer
Thought it scarcely worth his while
To waste much time on the old violin,
But held it up with a smile.
"What am I bidden, good folks?" he cried,
"Who'll start the bidding for me?"
"A dollar, a dollar. Then two! Only two?
Two dollars, and who'll make it three?"

Leverage Your Present Power

"Three dollars, once; three dollars, twice;
Going for three..." But no,
From the room, far back, a gray-haired man
Came forward and picked up the bow;
Then, wiping the dust from the old violin,
And tightening the loosened strings,
He played a melody pure and sweet,
As a caroling angel sings.

The music ceased, and the auctioneer,
With a voice that was quiet and low,
Said: "What am I bid for the old violin?"
And he held it up with the bow.
"A thousand dollars, and who'll make it two?
Two thousand! And who'll make it three?
Three thousand, once; three thousand, twice,
And going and gone," said he.

Leverage Your Present Power

The people cheered, but some of them cried,
"We do not quite understand.
What changed its worth?" Swift came the reply:
"The touch of the Master's hand."
And many a man with life out of tune,
And battered and scarred with sin,
Is auctioned cheap to the thoughtless crowd
Much like the old violin.

A "mess of pottage," a glass of wine,
A game — and he travels on.
He is "going" once, and "going" twice,
He's "going" and almost "gone."
But the Master comes, and the foolish crowd
Never can quite understand
The worth of a soul and the change that is wrought
By the touch of the Master's hand.

-Myra Brooks Welch

Leverage Your Present Power

This poem is one I heard often as a child. I have found myself researching and reading it repeatedly as I have gotten older as well. The poem never gets old to me. For I have been in the state of the old violin. I have been in situations where others attempted to convince me that I was diminished, tarnished, worn, and tired. In my weakness and immaturity, at times I believed them and began to feel that I was diminished, tarnished, worn, and tired. But I now understand that in those hard times and in those valley experiences, all it takes is the touch of someone who knows and can see our value and purpose. All it takes is one touch, one interaction, or one voice, and the value is unveiled.

There are many lessons within this one poem. But one key takeaway is that we have to be careful not to undervalue or undersell ourselves or others. It takes one touch, one choice, or one step to initiate the process of the transportation of transformation.

Leverage Your Present Power

The process of transformation begins internally. But it will be reflected externally. The transportation ignited through the touch of the master's hand can cause eyes that were once blind to your value and power to open and see you. The transformation that comes through the touch of the master's hand can cause ears that were once deafened to your voice, ideas, and concerns to open and hear your message. Transformation has a powerful impact both internally and externally.

In this book, we will focus on the internal process and impact of transformation. But the internal work we will undergo through the material covered in this book will have impacts externally, as well. As you transform internally, you will enter spaces differently. You will communicate differently. You will interact differently. Your external experiences will change because you are progressing internally.

Leverage Your Present Power

The transportation and movement of transformation are powerful. There are some key principles of movement that apply to this transportation of transformation. The four pairs of key principles are as follows:

1. Power & Strength
2. Speed & Momentum
3. Balance & Flexibility
4. Endurance & Perseverance

The first principle we will cover is power and strength. We will spend the rest of this chapter discussing our current power and strength.

Transformation can transport us from where we currently stand (our present power) to where we can be (our purposed potential).
As we take the journey through this book together, I would like to begin with the process of identifying, communicating, and leveraging the present power you currently possess.

Embrace Authenticity

Who am I? These three words formulate the most meaningful question, for which we must know the true and accurate response. Michelle Obama once said, "There's power in allowing yourself to be known and heard, in owning your unique story, in using your authentic voice." We must first know, in order to be known. To present ourselves authentically so that others may know us and hear us, we must first know ourselves, our message, and our voice. We have to fully understand who we are. The process of discovering and defining who we are includes removing the layers that we have socially constructed. We are removing these layers for a purpose. The purpose of removing these layers is to unleash the power we have inside.

The layers we have constructed were generally established for a reason. We often create layers by putting on mental or emotional personal protective equipment (PPE) to establish a sense of

Leverage Your Present Power

protection. The threat of mental or emotional harm may be real and would then substantiate the need for healthy boundaries. These layers and boundaries are often defense mechanisms to compensate for the perceived lack of safety.

There were likely situations and circumstances that triggered the need for this level of protection. Boundary setting is necessary and healthy. However, it is important to also note that these defense mechanisms are elements that have the potential to rob us of our freedom and identity. Therefore, to identify our authentic selves and authentic power, we must reunite identity, freedom, and safety. In this effort, it is critical to regularly examine ourselves to understand what constraints we may be operating within. The routine examination will enable us to determine if those constraints, boundaries, and limitations are still valid. If we do not regularly examine ourselves, we may find that we have layers of personal protective equipment that we no longer need. The threat of harm may no longer exist.

Even during the time when personal protective equipment is necessary, we must be careful not to lose sight of who we are underneath all the layers. It is the authentic person who takes the transformative journey we will undergo through the exercises and content covered in this book. The version of you that is created and demonstrated through your performance does not get to take this journey. The success of the transformative journey requires the identification of an accurate starting point. It cannot be the starting point we crafted or the starting point we are comfortable with. The starting point of the transformation must be the point at which you currently stand, in your authentic state of being.

In the Stanford Encyclopedia of Philosophy, the definition of authenticity is being faithful to the foundational being[1]. Another definition of authenticity is an unhindered, unconstrained existence[2]. As these definitions suggest, there are hindrances and constraints that attempt to cause us to defy who we are at our foundation.

Human beings are the only creatures that pretend to be something other than who they are. Cows do not pretend to be chickens. Dogs do not pretend to be elephants. They understand and embrace who and what they are. They behave in an authentic manner that is consistent with who they are.

It is interesting to realize that we are born fully willing and capable of living life authentically, free of limitations and pretenses. When toddlers are hungry, they will let you know, in the most authentic way possible, that they are hungry. If a young child is angry, they will let you know, in the most authentic way possible, that they are angry. At this early stage in life, we do not have a sense of constraints, limitations, or insecurities. Therefore, it would stand to reason that limitations and insecurities are learned.

Somewhere along our journey, the invitation to assume limitations and insecurities was offered, received, and accepted. There are many mechanisms in which this invitation can be offered. The invitation may come from others, from situations, or from ourselves. Pain or exhaustion make it easier to accept these invitations. Shame and guilt also make it easier to accept these invitations. If we succumb to the pain, exhaustion, shame, or guilt and believe the negative, inferior narratives written for us within this invitation; we will hide. We will hide those parts of ourselves that we deem to be unworthy, unlovable, or unforgivable. But these narratives are often untrue and are always incomplete. We are hiding parts of ourselves instead of walking the path of healing for

Leverage Your Present Power

ourselves. Whatever has transpired or whatever has been said; it is not final. We have the ability and power to grow, develop, and transport ourselves to a new state through the power of transformation.

Regardless of where the invitation comes from, we have a choice of whether we wish to accept it. We can choose to sacrifice our authentic selves, our authentic beliefs, and our authentic dreams to assume the identity that fits within the constraints and limitations offered to us. Or, we can choose another option. We have the ability to reject the invitation for limitations and instead focus and activate the power in our leverage to move. Leverage is defined as the ability to utilize strengths to produce improved outcomes or diminish costs and risks[7]. We can choose to activate the authentic strengths and power we have to transform ourselves and transcend the limitations offered by others. The limitations offered by others often

Leverage Your Present Power

restrain the power and strength we have within our authentic beings.

We can make the choice to be authentically who we are. There is power in being rather than seeming. In 1893, the North Carolina General Assembly established its state motto, which is "Esse Quam Videri.[4]" This is a Latin phrase that means "to be, rather than to seem." This motto amplifies the message of authenticity. Søren Kierkegaard, a Danish philosopher, urges people to "become what one is." This suggests that there is an evolution in authenticity. As we experience life, we discover and learn more about ourselves. We must then have the grit and boldness to remain faithful to what we ascertain regarding our authentic being. This evolutionary process allows us to complete the statement of the North Carolina state motto in a positive way. To be, rather than to seem, is liberating. To be, rather than to seem, is empowering. To be, rather than to seem, is purposeful.

Leverage Your Present Power

However, it is important to recognize that in the beginning stages of the process of identifying who we are, the completion of the statement may not be as positive. To be, rather than to seem, can be scary. To be, rather than to seem, can be lonely. To be, rather than to seem, can be costly. When your authentic being is different from what you have been taught is normal or acceptable, it can be scary. When your authentic being is unique among those around you, it can be a lonely place. When your authentic being is in contrast to or conflict with the comfort of others, it can be costly.

I have learned in life that there are some costs that are worth paying for. In this case, the return is necessary. The benefits gained exceed the weight of the costs. For the benefits of reuniting freedom, identity, and safety far outweigh the costs of disrupting toxic comfort. I have experienced situations where I paid the price for disrupting the toxic comfort within an existing environment. The reaction I endured from others was hard and painful. But the purpose of my process of respectfully shifting mindsets and disrupting the unhealthy soil in which others were planted was necessary. It was necessary so that others who came after me did not have to pay as high of a cost. The manner in which we undergo the process of shifting mindsets matters. We must maintain respect and give grace. I am grateful for those who came before me and paid the price of disrupting others' toxic comfort. I repay their sacrifice by paying it forward to those I have the opportunity to lift, as I climb.

The evolutionary process of authenticity is comprised of four steps[2]:

1. Self-Awareness
2. Non-judgmental Reflection
3. Behavioral Alignment
4. Relational Alignment

Leverage Your Present Power

The first step to authenticity is self-awareness. This step involves the recognition of our thoughts, beliefs, values, instincts, and emotions. We must separate the thoughts, beliefs, values, instincts, and emotions of others from our own. It is easy to unconsciously assume the qualities of others. But to get to the core of who we are, we have to be able to distinguish our thoughts from the thoughts others place in our minds. We need to be able to separate our beliefs from those that seem to be the most common or acceptable. We must be able to delineate our values from the values we were told to have. We need to be able to separate our instincts and true emotions from our restrained and conditioned responses.

In the second step of the process, we progress from recognition to understanding. We are complex beings. To gain a full understanding of all the facets and dimensions of who we are, we must courageously reflect on the total picture of who we are. This enables us to identify the reasons and motivations behind the thoughts, beliefs, values, instincts, and emotions we identified in step one.

When the FBI is training agents to recognize counterfeit currency, they do not begin by having the agents study all the techniques counterfeiters use to deceive merchants. They have the agents study the genuine currency[32]. They have them study the real money until they know every intricate detail of it. This enables them to recognize if anything is presented to them that does not align with what they know to be real. Similarly, we have to take the time to study ourselves. We have to know who we are. We must know every intricate detail – every strength and every struggle, every triumph and every trigger, every gift and every gap. Once you fully know who you are, when you are presented with anything that paints a picture of you that is less than who you are, you will recognize it for what it is – deception. The process of learning who you are is one to enjoy and cherish.

In gaining this understanding of the many facets of who we are and the drivers behind who we are, we can now move to step three: aligning our behavior to who we are. It is in this step that we will drop the award-winning performances that we tend to give on a day-to-day, situation-by-situation basis.

Are there aspects of your habits and routines that do not align with your beliefs and values? If so, what is stopping you from exercising the courage to change those behaviors to create alignment? How might you mitigate those obstacles to achieving alignment? What is one step you can take towards gaining the alignment between your beliefs, values, and actions? Let's commit to making that step today.

Personally, once I realized what was inside of me, I was able to change my behaviors and actions. I stopped looking for the light at the end of the tunnel once I realized that I was the light. I am the solution I was searching for. The solution was inside of me.

As we align our behaviors, we can align our relationships accordingly as well. Are your friends connecting and enjoying your company, or are they experiencing a masterful performance that is different from who you are authentically? Has your partner fallen in love with you, or are they in love with a version of you that you have created? Living life unauthentically is exhausting and unfulfilling for you and for those around you.

You own your story. You add dimension to your story that no one else can provide. Someone else may write, "She woke up, got ready to go, then went to work." But with your unique perspective, you would write it differently.

Your perspective provides layers of details and feelings that cannot be told from an outside view. You would write and tell the story with more meaning. "With the heaviness of a night filled with paralyzing fears and unsolved issues on her mind, she opened her eyes. She mustered all the strength she had to rise from a prostrate position to one where she was seated in bed. She eventually found the strength to stand. Standing has not always been easy. So the ability to stand provided a sense of gratitude and shifted her mindset. Though she was overcome with the responsibilities of the day ahead, she knew she had a purpose that must be fulfilled. She knew she had something to give. She knew she had those that she was called to serve. She recognized that the purpose and potential of the day overshadowed the pain of the night before. This recognition enabled her to press forward and claim her day as her own."

Do not release the power of your story to someone else to tell. It is your story, your power, and your strength. As we grow in our authenticity, we will unveil, embrace, and leverage our strengths. To identify your strengths, think back to when you were a child.

1. What types of things did you enjoy doing most?
2. Did you enjoy activities where you were interacting with others?
3. Did you enjoy activities where you had the freedom to create and build?
4. Did you enjoy adventurous activities?
5. Did you find joy in solving puzzles or riddles?

Now, let's think more recently. Reflect on the past few years.

Leverage Your Present Power

1. What have you spent the most time dreaming or thinking about?
2. What groups of people are you led to help?
3. What problems are you drawn to solving? What issues in the world agitate you the most?
4. In what ways are you unique? Your uniqueness is often your superpower.
5. What do people compliment you about the most?
6. In which situations did you experience the most joy or fulfillment?
7. What types of actions and interactions were happening in this situation?

As you review the responses to these questions, themes may emerge that will help you pinpoint the strengths you have. Your strengths are only part of your power. There is power in your presence. There is power in your

Leverage Your Present Power

purpose. There is power in your story. There is power in your overcoming. There is power in you.

The next step is to go from identifying and understanding our present power to having the ability to communicate that power.

There is a difference between self-identity and personal brand. Self-identity is how you identify and see yourself. Your personal brand is how others see and experience you. Ideally, there will be alignment between your identity and your personal brand. There is power in self-identity. If you believe strongly enough in who you are, it will show in your thoughts, words, actions, and habits. Your thoughts, words, actions, and habits will then begin to formulate your brand.

If we take a lion as an example, a lion is not the biggest animal in the jungle. A lion is not the fastest animal in the jungle. But the lion is the king of the jungle *(or more accurately, the savanna)* because he believes he is the king[31]. He believes it so strongly that he walks like he is king. He roars like a king. The other animals that are bigger, stronger, and faster than the lion respect the lion as king. The lion's self-identity is so strong that it has become his personal brand.

This is where the power of belief comes into play. There is an adage that states, "Seeing is believing." But I must honestly say that what I have seen in my life is the reverse. If I believe it strongly enough, I know I will see it. For I will not stop working, striving, learning, and growing until I see it.

What is your self-identity? Can you communicate your purpose, passion, and power? We often craft sales pitches about something we want someone to believe in. But how much more important is it to be able to clearly communicate your purpose, power, and value? Not necessarily for others, but it

Leverage Your Present Power

is important for you to be able to communicate this to yourself. Maya Angelou once said, "People will very often try to respond to you on the level on which you address them." This also applies to how we speak to ourselves. What thoughts do you have about yourself? What are you communicating with your inner voice? The ability to communicate purpose, power, and value is a critical skill to learn.

This ability to communicate our power is important because there are many forces in this world that will *attempt*, in various ways, to diminish your perception of the power you possess. Notice I said these forces *attempt* to diminish your perception. Nothing external can diminish your actual value. If it did not create you, then it cannot contain you. If it did not design you, it cannot deny you. So you have to know your value, without a doubt. You have to know your power. Know who you are.

Leverage Your Present Power

In the movie *Black Panther*, based on the Marvel comic book series, the point of self-identity and power is made. At one point in the movie, it was Challenge Day. This was a time when others deemed worthy could attempt to take the place of the king. During the challenge day battle, it appeared the current king, King T'Challa, was beginning to lose the fight. He was bloodied, and he was wounded. But at that moment, his mother yelled out, "Show them who you are!" This exclamation from his mother seemed to give him the reminder he needed to rise and defeat the challenger. He knew that he had the strength inside of him to overthrow his opponent. Despite his current state, circumstance, and condition, he was able to recall and demonstrate who he was.

In life, we can go through different challenges and obstacles. We battled through it. We fought the good fight. But in the end, we find ourselves left bloodied and wounded. You may know who you are. Yet in this season, the way you feel may be in contradiction with who you know yourself to be. You may believe you are smart and experienced. Yet when you are turned down for a position you know you are more than qualified for; you may begin to feel in a way that conflicts with your belief that you are smart and experienced. I know I am not just a conqueror. But I am more than a conqueror. Yet in certain situations, I was left feeling defeated.

When I was younger, I was in Girl Scouts. The mission of Girl Scouts is to build girls of courage, confidence, and character, who make the world a better place. When I unpack this mission, I find a critical connection in the three characteristics of character, confidence, and courage. They are building blocks.

Character is found in the answer to the question, "Who are you?" What are the characteristics that reflect who you are? This is your power. Confidence comes from believing that you have this power. Confidence is believing in yourself and in the power and purpose of your presence. Courage is the ability to be persistent in believing in yourself, even when it gets hard and even when you are scared. Even if others don't believe in you, courage is the audacity (*one of my favorite words*) to believe in yourself anyway. As we identify the beauty of who we are and the power of who we are, we must develop confidence in who we are. We must continue to affirm and build that confidence so that it facilitates courage. We will then have the courage to believe in the face of doubt or conflicting circumstances.

We all have areas we can improve. As we find them and address them, it makes us stronger. On this transformative journey, you will get better. You will grow and transform into a better version of yourself. But it is of utmost importance to know, as stated at the beginning of this chapter, that the current version of you has value and has something to offer this world. You can bloom where you are planted while you are reaching towards the sky. It is your time. It is always your time. Your time is now.

Leverage Your Present Power
At every stage and place in life, we not only have something to gain, but we also have something to contribute. An indigenous artist, named Nicholas Galanin spoke about this point by saying, "Use your own unique perspective and try to contribute, and not just consume." James Baldwin had a similar perspective when he stated, "The world is before you, and you need not take it or leave it as it was when you came in." At a foundational level, the word power refers to the capacity and ability to produce an effect. I personally think of power in terms of impact and influence. These definitions fit a number of aspects and uses of the word "power."

Leverage Your Present Power

There are many uses of the word power that correlate to the power we exhibit and use in our lives. One such use of the word, which also ties to the earlier example of the battery, refers to electrical power. The foundational definition holds true in this use of the word as well. Electrical power indeed demonstrates the capacity and ability to produce a specific effect – lights turn on, appliances function, etc. There are three primary functions that exist within the electrical power system. These functions are generation, transmission, and distribution.

The generation of power refers to the ability to source energy. The combination of energy and power is a necessary connection. The ability to source energy is a necessary function in the effort to understand, assess, grow, and transform someone's power. It is critical to identify where you gain energy.

Leverage Your Present Power

When you reflect on your life's journey, it will often reveal a source of power. There is a fuel that propels you forward in the face of adversity. You may not be able to recall all the details of various instances where you felt a surge of energy or power. But, reflect on what you felt in the moment. As Maya Angelou taught, "I've learned that people will forget what you said, people will forget what you did, but people will never forget how you made them feel." In the preface to his book, *Evidence of Things Not Seen*, James Baldwin concurs, as he states, "My memory stammers, but my soul is a witness."

Think of the times you felt the most inspired and determined. In those moments, can you pinpoint the source of energy and fuel?

Consider these questions:

1. What time of day do you have the most energy?
2. When are you most fulfilled?

Leverage Your Present Power

3. What types of conversations or experiences leave you feeling inspired and motivated?
4. In contrast, what types of conversations or experiences leave you feeling drained or disengaged?
5. How much time do you spend engaging in those activities that energize you compared to the time you spend engaging in the activities that drain you?

Once you identify the sources of your energy and fuel, intentionally create space and time to engage in those things. As you travel the journey of transformation, monitor the consistency and frequency with which you connect to your energy sources.

When you think of an electronic device, such as a mobile phone, the battery must be charged for it to function properly. When you use various applications and functions, it drains the battery, and eventually it will

Leverage Your Present Power

need to be recharged. Otherwise, it will shut down. Our lives work in a similar fashion. The more we use our strengths, gifts, and power, the more we endure challenges and obstacles; the more battles we have to fight and storms we have to endure, the more it can drain us of our energy. We need to recharge. So it is important to be aware of the types of activities and conversations that will recharge us. If we recognize that the frequency of our recharging activities is insufficient, an adjustment is necessary. With every new destination of growth and development comes the need to review, assess, and modify our schedule and the way in which we leverage our twenty-four hours each day.

The second function within the electrical power system is transmission. The transmission of power refers to the way in which the power is transported. When applied to our lives, this element of the power system answers the question, "How do you carry your

Leverage Your Present Power

power?" As it relates to this function of transmission, consider these questions:

1. Once you access energy, what do you do with it?
2. How far do you transmit the energy and power? Do you keep it to yourself or use it to empower others? Is the energy and power you gain used to serve yourself only, or is it used in the service of others as well?
3. Who do you serve? What groups of people would benefit the most from your gifts, strengths, and lessons from my story?
4. In what arenas and forums do you activate and leverage your strengths to serve others?
5. How wide is your current sphere of influence?

The transmission components align with the level of influence you have. It depicts the breadth of your impact.

Leverage Your Present Power

The third function of the power system is distribution. The distribution of power refers to someone's ability to distribute the appropriate level of energy and power to meet the needs of those who need it. There is an appropriate level of energy and power that should be applied to various people and spaces. The appropriateness of the energy level is determined by the nature of the relationship and engagement. Certain interactions and relationships may substantiate a high level of energy due to the need for trust, vulnerability, and closeness. Other relationships may not substantiate the same level of energy investment.

The ability to discern the appropriate level of need and the appropriate level of safety is essential to achieving and maintaining emotional balance. The energy and power you distribute may not be equal for every recipient or person with whom you interact. Not everyone should have access beyond the veil. There are some levels of energy and power that are held for only a select group of individuals, and the level of energy distributed will translate to the effective use of the power provided by that energy. The distribution component aligns with the level and depth of the impact you have.

The way in which we leverage our power aligns with these three main functions of the power system: power generation, power transmission, and power distribution. As we generate power, it is not for us to hide that power. The power we obtain is obtained for a reason. If we earn a place in the room or a seat at the table, we must make our presence count. It is not enough to have power. We must come out of hiding and use the strength and power we have.

Hide and Seek
When my daughter was four years old, I went to pick her up from her preschool class, and her teacher

informed me that all the children were outside playing hide and seek. I went outside, and the children were all huddled around the middle of the playground. Then one of the kids started to count. 1…2…3…. At once, all the children scattered across the playground to find the most optimal hiding spots.

One kid went and hid behind this huge oak tree. Another child went and hid behind a piece of playground equipment. But then I see my child standing right in the middle of the playground, directly in front of the child counting, and she has her arms folded.

I immediately thought, "Oh, they did not tell my baby how to play the game." So I yelled across the playground and said, "Sweetie, you are supposed to run and hide when he is counting. Then he will try to find you when he is finished counting."

Leverage Your Present Power

My daughter instantly looked back at me and responded, "No ma'am. Last time they were counting, I went and hid, and no one came to seek me. So this time I'm going to stand right here, and they are going to have to reckon with me." Now I did not know what the words "they are going to have to reckon with me" meant coming from a four-year-old. Nevertheless, her response made me reflect on my own life and the lives of those around me.

How often do we hide when it counts? How often do we find ourselves hiding behind insecurities, hiding behind titles, hiding behind other people's comfort, hiding behind generational patterns, and waiting for someone to come search for us?

It is time to stop hiding our gifts and talents. We have to stop hiding who we are. Come out, come out wherever you are. Come to the center. Stand your ground and say, "They are going to have to reckon with me." You were

Leverage Your Present Power

created to be an answer. Do not hold your answers and solutions back. Know your value, so you can own your value. Regardless of where you come from or what you have been through, there is power in your journey. Your journey created something within you that your family, your community, and this world need.

YOU HAVE VALUE.
YOU HAVE POWER.
YOU HAVE WORTH.
YOU HAVE WINGS.
USE THEM.
Start today. Let's soar.

2

Activate Your Motivation to Move

Stepping into your present power and leveraging that power to make positive internal and external change is an incredible feeling. It is fulfilling and rewarding. Yet there is more! There is more for you to gain. There is more for you to give.

In the movie The Lion King, the father lion, named Mufasa, provides words of wisdom to his son, Simba. He says to him, "Look inside yourself. You are more than what you have become." This quotation highlights the importance of not settling for your present power or your current list of accomplishments. It is important that

Activate Your Motivation to Move

you discover and live within the purpose for which you were created. A purpose is an abiding cause or goal to which focused effort is applied. In our lives, we must do more than exist. We must do more than remain at one level of growth and development. We must continuously move towards our purposed potential.

As mentioned in the previous chapter, there are four key sets of principles of movement:

1. Power & Strength
2. Speed & Momentum
3. Balance & Flexibility
4. Endurance & Perseverance

We covered power and strength in the previous chapter. The next set of principles are speed and momentum. There are multiple factors that determine the speed at which we are able to transform. However, our growth and development enable us to be ready when the need and opportunity for transformation arise. As we experience in life, the appropriate speed is dependent on the driver. An experienced driver of a vehicle can drive at 60 or 70 mph without problems. However, that same speed for a new driver would be dangerous. The driver must have sufficient vision to determine the appropriate path. The driver must have the focus, clarity, and strength to change directions when necessary. The driver must also maintain clarity and direction along the journey. The driver must also have the motivation to maintain momentum. Speed comes through vision, clarity, and momentum.

Vision
As we progress forward, and before we build up momentum, we need to know where we are going. We need to identify the next destination on our journey to our purposed potential.

If we reflect on and unpack our life thus far, we will reveal themes that point us to our purpose. We were created on purpose and for a purpose. For us to transport from our present power to our purposed potential, we must be able to identify our purpose. Understanding our purpose and passion gives us the foundation we need to communicate and optimize the power and beauty of who we are.

When organizations are formed, the owners of the enterprise define a clear purpose for the organization. The organizational core values, decisions, and work align with that purpose. The organizational purpose helps those working with and for the organization to focus their efforts, and collectively drive towards goals. In the same way that a defined purpose works for an organization, understanding your personal purpose will help to focus your efforts as you travel the path of transformation from your present power to your purposed potential.

Activate Your Motivation to Move

As you reflect on your life's journey, you will identify the themes within your experiences that may unlock your purpose. To reflect means to bounce back without absorbing. Therefore, if done appropriately, reflection is a process of reviewing the past to learn and appreciate. Reflection is not a process in which you absorb the negativity from past situations. There is life-altering power in the phrase, "My past is not a prison. My past is a school." As long as we take that approach, the act of reflection is a positive action that will reap fruitful results.

We are reflecting on our life's journey for the purpose of understanding our story so that we can ascertain our purpose and our power. Our purpose is not limited to our skills or functions; our purpose is found within our story. Each experience, every triumph, and every challenge prepares you for your purpose.

Activate Your Motivation to Move

This is a lesson I learned early in life. When I reflect on my life, I see an evolution of purpose. The first stage of purpose I see in my life is purpose as defined by others. When we are children and do not yet have the level of experience to differentiate our exceptional gifts from our challenges, we are left to others' interpretation of the purpose of our lives. People would notice what I was capable of doing, and they would craft a purpose for me based on the skillset they had witnessed. I was excellent with numbers. I was an outstanding student. I was also talented in sports. I was creative. Therefore, my purpose was crafted around my functions within those areas. Some told me I would be an engineer or an accountant due to my skill with numbers. Some told me I would be an Olympic gymnast due to my abilities in the sport. Others told me I would be a concert pianist or a designer due to my creativity. This phase of purpose evolution was not fulfilling for me, as my purpose as defined by others always felt limiting.

The next phase of the evolution of purpose in my life was understanding the agility of purpose. One of the most important lessons I have learned is that purpose is not static and is not confined to one time period or one area within your life. This is the phase where I truly came to realize that my purpose was not tied to my skills. My purpose was tied to my story. I was a gymnast for many years. But I came to a point where my gymnastics career was over. Now what? Who am I now, since I am no longer Endya the gymnast? Because I had attached my identity to my function, once that function was removed, I was lost.

It was at this point that I had to spend a lot of time diving into my life experiences. I had to take a close look at my successes. I also had to dive deeply into my fears, choices, and challenges. Honestly, it was my challenges that taught me the most about my strengths. I am far from being arrogant. In fact, I dealt with low self-esteem for many years. There were several years of my life where I believed the negativity and doubts that were spoken to me and around me. I often felt I did not measure up to where I should or could be. However, I now know who I am.

It was not until I explored all I had faced and all I had overcome that I realized that there was a fire and a power within me that allowed me to overcome. There was something inside of me that gave me the strength to stand when standing was not easy. There was something inside of me that gave me the courage to press forward in the face of doubters. There was something inside of me that gave me the audacity to believe that if my back is against the wall, I can muster up the strength to tear that wall down to get to the other side. There was a strength within me that I had to identify, embrace, and unleash.

When people ask me who I am, I am aware they are expecting the response to be my job title and employment status. But when I respond, I am now aware that who I am is not confined to a title. Who I am is the impact I make on the world.

I am a transformational leader. When I lead, transformation happens. I am a courageous warrior who was forged in the fire. So I will not shy away when the situation gets hot and the flames are high. My journey has given me a level of fire, passion, and determination that sets me apart. I am uniquely positioned to see value and gifting in people, even when they are unable to see it in themselves. I am equipped to partner with and guide people on the transformative journey to fulfill the value and potential of their lives. When I step into a room, hope, inspiration, and breakthroughs come with me.

Activate Your Motivation to Move

I was created to address issues surrounding those who are broken, lost, or looking for more, with the purpose of helping them gain clarity and transformation in their lives. That is who I am. Regardless of my job title, role, or location, this is who I am. This is what those I encounter will experience.

One of the many lessons I learned from my mother is that no one should ever enter your presence hungry and not leave full. That is physically, emotionally, and mentally applicable. I seek to feed the hungry. That is what I was created to do. That is my purpose.

The final stage in the evolution of purpose is to distinguish between being capable and being called. To be capable means to possess the necessary mindset, skillset, and toolset to complete a mission or task. To be called means to be uniquely positioned and purposed for a mission and task. At various stages in life, there will be multiple things that you are capable of doing well. In those seasons, it is important to note that your ability to do something well does not mean that it is the best action for you to take. By taking on more than you are called to take on, you invite unnecessary stress by assuming someone else's responsibility. By stepping outside of your current area of calling, you also rob others of the opportunity to grow and develop. Clarity of purpose and strength of discernment are necessary at this stage. The actions you choose to take and the goals you choose to pursue must align with your purpose for this leg of your journey.

Another component of vision is the importance of assessing and understanding *how* we see. This is the point where we can pinpoint any issues within our vision that we need to address before embarking on our transformative journey.

Optically speaking, our vision is determined by the manner in which our eyes focus and bend light onto our retinas. Two conditions, nearsightedness and farsightedness, are determined by the improper diversion of light[20]. Nearsightedness refers to a condition wherein an individual sees closer objects with more clarity and focus than objects that are farther away. Wherein farsighted individuals see objects farther away with more clarity and focus than they do objects that are closer. With each of these conditions, light still flows into the eye, and pictures and information are still captured by the brain. However, the outcome is a lack of clarity in the vision. Both of these conditions are associated with strain and pain[21]. But they both can be mitigated through the use of corrective lenses or a procedure to alter the shape of the eye, thereby correcting one's vision.

The way in which our eyes formulate vision correlates to the components

Activate Your Motivation to Move

and factors impacting vision in our lives. Through various experiences, we are capturing information. However, in examining our perspective, we may find we are nearsighted. We may have a clear understanding and vision of the events occurring in the present and in the near future. But when we have to cast our faith and belief into things beyond the horizon, we may find we have a lack of clarity and focus on events that are in a more distant future. With our attention firmly fixed on the present state, it causes strain and pain to let go of what we see clearly today to be able to cast a vision and dream of what may be in the future. At times, the struggle and pain that exist in the past and in the present can cause the future to be blurry and out of view.

It is also possible, when examining your vision, to notice that you have no issue clearly seeing the desired future destination, no matter how far it may be, but you have a lack of clarity of the present state and the space in between.

Activate Your Motivation to Move

There are also many reasons this condition may exist. It can be easier to focus on a distant, bright future when the present and past have been dark and hard. It is the art of tempting to avoid, ignore, or numb the pain of today to try to reach for something else.

In addition to nearsightedness and farsightedness, we can also develop blind spots. Many issues can create blind spots. Unhealed wounds from the past can create areas we are not willing to face. These areas would be blind spots. Biases can create blind spots. Biases are sometimes taught. Sometimes biases result from our experiences. But they can also create blind spots.

Just as corrective lenses can be used to counteract nearsightedness and farsightedness, there are tools that can be used to correct our vision. One corrective lens that we can use is to reframe or adjust the story we tell

Activate Your Motivation to Move

ourselves about the past. We can leverage this corrective lens to combat nearsightedness and farsightedness. We will go into reframing in more detail soon.

A corrective lens that can address various blind spots is perspective taking. Henry David Thoreau once asked, "Could a greater miracle take place than for us to look through each other's eyes for an instant?"

In transportation, a blind spot is defined as an area in which the scope of vision is restricted[25]. Many things may restrict vision during transportation. Parts of the vehicle or our cargo can be in the way of our field of vision. Is there something you are carrying that is restricting your vision? Is there something too big or causing too much worry for you to cast your vision more broadly? Assess whether the load you are carrying is truly yours to carry. Ensure you haven't picked up something that belongs to someone

Activate Your Motivation to Move

else. Is it someone else's responsibility that you have taken on yourself, which is now keeping you from seeing your destiny clearly?

The size of the mirror and reflection can also restrict the vision[25]. What is the scope of your reflection and your vision? Are you willing to look at all the options and possibilities? Another factor that can cause blind spots is the distance from the mirror or reflection. How often are you spending time reflecting on your day, your life, and your surroundings?

In driving, to correct blind spots, the first step is to identify the blind spots. Once the blind spots are identified, the mirrors must be cleared and adjusted to compensate for the space that is not seen. It is helpful to have a team, a corner, or a personal advisory board that may be able to see things that you cannot. This should be a group of trusted individuals who have the ability and willingness to help you grow and develop in the areas you are looking to transform.

Clarity and Direction
Clarity comes from the alignment of your purpose with your dreams, thoughts, beliefs, values, instincts, and emotions. This alignment brings about confirmation. As you confirm your overall purpose, additional clarity comes with the refinement of your purpose.

When we unpack our story, we will reveal the power of who we are. When you reflect on your life, what themes do you see? Do you see themes of strength, resiliency, learning, or the ability to leverage opportunities?

Consider these questions:

1. When you reflect on your successes, what would you say was your greatest success?
2. What components of the success or the journey to the success

made it stand out above the other accomplishments in your life?
3. When you reflect on your challenges, what was the most difficult challenge you faced?
4. What lesson did you learn from the challenge that you now carry with you? How did you overcome it?

By identifying how you overcame your greatest challenges, you will uncover a strength or a superpower that you possess. Something inside of you enabled you to overcome that challenge and learn from it. Even if it is a challenge you are still facing, you are still standing. That means something. It means you are stronger than whatever you are facing.

Understanding your purpose and passion will bring clarity to your life's journey. Your purpose and passion will serve as a compass to guide your future steps. Your purpose will directly align with your dreams, thoughts, beliefs, values, instincts, and emotions.

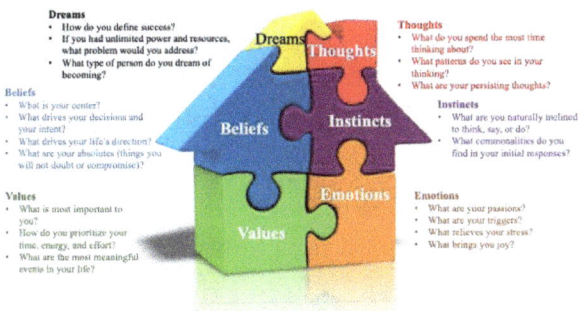

Consider the questions outlined in the diagram above and listed below:

Dreams
- How do you define success?
- If you had unlimited power and resources, what problem would you address?
- What type of person do you dream of becoming?

Thoughts
- What do you spend the most time thinking about?

- What patterns do you see in your thinking?
- What are your persisting thoughts – those thoughts that continue to make it to the forefront of your mind?

Beliefs
- What is your center?
- What drives your decisions and your intent?
- What drives your life's direction?
- What are your absolutes (things you will not doubt or compromise)?

Instincts
- What are you naturally inclined to think, say, or do?
- What commonalities do you find in your initial responses?

Values
- What is most important to you?
- How do you prioritize your time, energy, and effort?

- What are the most meaningful events in your life?

Emotions
- What are your passions?
- What are your triggers?
- What relieves your stress?
- What brings you joy?

Capture the recurring themes you see in your responses. These themes will help you to gain clarity within the vision of your purpose.

What within this current season of your life are you able to do in working towards your purposed potential? When you take an inventory of the strength, power, and privilege you have, you must ask yourself two questions:

1. What am I doing with my current strength, power, and privilege?

2. What could I be doing with my current strength, power, and privilege?

The gap in these two questions can bring clarity to the purposed work in which you can take steps to complete. Along this transformative journey, you will be working within your purpose and gaining fruitful results all along the way.

Obtaining and maintaining clarity and direction requires focus and strength. My favorite definition of focus is selective attention. There are many things, in which we can choose to apply our focus. Our focus and attention have value. Therefore, we choose what we *pay* our attention and focus to. Ensure that whatever you choose to pay your attention and focus to are worthy of it. It is important to set a standard for what you choose to focus on. It is then important to have a method of determining what item to focus on and when.

Activate Your Motivation to Move

When you set a standard, you are establishing key criteria, or the bare minimum that would be acceptable. Not everything deserves your attention. Consistent negativity does not deserve your attention. Doubt is not worthy of your focus. Disrespect has not earned your attention. Excuses are not worth your focus. Set your standards of what qualifies as acceptable for focus time and what does not qualify.

Boundaries are a powerful tool to setting standards. It is also important that you take the next step in boundary setting. Once you set your boundary, make that boundary clear and apparent to others. Thirdly, you must honor your boundary by maintaining your standards. When you respond by saying, "no" to a futile request for your time and attention; you are simply making room to say, "yes" to the right things. Saying no allows you to be available for the activities that align with your purpose. It will keep you from having to say no to purposeful activities because you are too busy with activities that are distracting you from your purpose and transformative journey.

This takes strength. No is a one syllable word. But at times, it takes a lot of strength to say it. One thing my husband shared with our children when they were young was, "always have something better to do." This is very wise counsel. When offers come to you that do not meet your standard for your focus and attention, always have something better to do. It is easier to respond by saying "No, I cannot commit to your request, as I have some preparation to do in my field of purpose." There is always work you can do to prepare for and while on your transformation journey. You will always have the option of having something better to do, as you are moving towards the better version of yourself.

It is also critical to recognize when you may have strayed from the original course to the desired destination. When driving down a road, if you recognize that you are headed north when you should be headed south, you have to make a U-turn. The longer you wait to turn around the longer it will take you to get to the desired destination. It is the same way in life. When we recognize that our thoughts, words, or actions are resulting in fruit that is not what we intended, then we have to disrupt the soil in which we are planted and start again. The quicker we recognize the wrong direction, identify the issue, address the issue, and change direction, the better.

Momentum
The law of inertia, which is Newton's first law of motion, states that an object at rest will stay at rest; and an object in motion will stay in motion, until it encounters an external force[8]. When it comes to the transportation of transformation, to go from a state of rest, comfort, or stagnation to a state of forward momentum, there must be a

force propelling you forward. That force will come through inspiration and motivation.

Newton's second law of motion, the law of force, states that the speed of an object is determined by the object's mass and the amount of force applied to it[9]. Our mass would translate to the power and purposed potential we are currently carrying inside. The amount of force will be determined by the intensity and depth of the inspiration and motivation we possess.

To prepare for the transportation of transformation, we must be motivated and inspired to move. The definition of inspire is to fill someone with the desire and force to act or move. The word motivation refers to providing someone with the motive or reason to act or move. Inspiration provides the desire and force. Motivation provides the motive and reason.

Activate Your Motivation to Move

To transform we must be willing to exit our current state in order to enter our phase of transformation. To confidently and determinedly make the choice to transform, the purpose or potential in the destination must be greater than the comfort of the existing place.

We must press our way through comfort and complacency and refuse to settle for less than our potential. We cannot settle for less than the best version of ourselves that we can be. As George Bernard Shaw pointed out, there are three kinds of people in this world:

1. Those who make things happen
2. Those who watch what happens
3. Those who wonder what happened

We have a choice as to what type of person we choose to be. Which of the three categories of people do you fall within today? In which of the three categories of people would you choose

Activate Your Motivation to Move

to belong? Bruce Lee once said "what you are not changing, you are choosing." Choose to improve. Choose to progress. Choose to optimize. Choose to make things happen. We must be able to boldly declare that "I am here in this place and in this state for a season; and I will optimize my purpose and power within this season. But my current place, "here", is not where I will stay. I am exercising the transportation of transformation to become the best version of me."

When he was younger, my son Jax loved the cartoon called Transformers. The cartoon was about robots who were able to fight battles on the ground. But if the situation or challenge required them to elevate to a different level or to move at a different pace; the robots had the ability to transform into another form that allowed them to meet the challenge in front of them. They generally transformed into various forms of transportation such as planes, cars, or trucks.

Activate Your Motivation to Move

The theme song included the line "Transformers more than meets the eye." At first glance, the robots may appear one way. But there was so much more that they could do. There was so much more that they were.

In watching the show with my son thousands of times, and hearing that theme song almost every day; I found myself singing it at random times. There were a number of times where I found myself facing challenging predicaments. It would be easy in those moments to throw my hands up and say I am not able to accomplish this goal. But I had to realize that I have the ability to transform. I came to realize that the situation may look overwhelming, but there was more to it than meets the eye. There was also more to me than meets the eye. Through transformation, I can travel from a place of "I am not able to" to a destination of "I already did."

Activate Your Motivation to Move

No matter how dark the place is where you start, transportation through transformation is possible. An artist named Terri St Cloud was working with a less experienced artist who had made an error in her painting. When speaking of this artist Terri said, "She could never go back and make some of the details pretty. All she could do was move forward and make the whole thing beautiful."

We all have parts of our journey we wish we could erase. We cannot change our past. However, we can move forward and realize that we are all beautiful masterpieces. Every mistake, every wrong turn, every blemish can be leveraged in the overall canvas of your life to make it beautiful. The jazz musician Miles Davis once said "If you hit a wrong note, it's the next note that makes it good or bad." Dark skies do not always mean rain. We must continue to grow, develop, and transform; knowing we are becoming the masterpieces we were created to be.

Activate Your Motivation to Move

One concept that is helpful in this motivation to continue to move forward is to create an exit strategy for each stage of your developmental journey. What do you seek to give to and to gain from your current place? What will you seek to add to your mindset, skillset, and toolset? What gifts and talents do you intend to leverage to make a positive impact during this stage? You have something to give, and something to learn in every stage of life in which you enter. It is helpful to be intentional regarding the creation of a strategy to ensure you get and give the most out of each opportunity and each stage of life.

Creating this strategy defines a purpose for each stage. It is similar to going to a restaurant to eat. Let's say you are hungry; and you have decided to go to a specific restaurant to eat. You are not going to leave the restaurant without getting what you came for and giving the appropriate payment for it.

Activate Your Motivation to Move

You would not go to a restaurant and pay for your meal, without receiving the food. Thus you should not enter into a stage in life, or a new role, and give all you have to it; only leave without receiving something in return. Similarly, you would not go to restaurant, and eat a full meal; then walk out without providing payment for the meal you received. It therefore follows that you should not enter into a stage in life, receiving from it, but not contributing to it. In various roles or positions, you will receive new knowledge, connections, and expertise. In those same roles or positions, you should a leverage your mindset, skillset, and toolset to contribute to the work and the people you have the opportunity to impact in that stage.

Your exit strategy is a living and breathing strategy. As you operate within your current state you will become aware of additional things you can gain from that place. *Gain* all you can from the place where you currently

Activate Your Motivation to Move

stand. *Give* all you can to the place where you currently stand.

Ensuring you have optimized the place in which you currently stand will help to facilitate your exit from the current state. It will also help to prepare you for the entrance into your next state. It will aid you in ensuring you do not become bitter. Instead, you will become better. You will not focus on what may have been toxic or less than optimal in your current state. You can choose to focus on what you gained from that place. What did it build within you that will help you on your journey? This will enable you to transform bitterness to gratefulness.

In addition to having vision, clarity, and momentum, it is important for the driver to know the vehicle used for transportation.

Transformation Vehicle
One framework I leverage to examine where I am and where I need to

develop consists of three main components. These components are the fuel which propel you forward. The three components within this framework are:

1. Mindset
2. Skillset
3. Toolset

I refer to this framework as fuel because each component within the framework must be assessed frequently. If you find that you are no longer moving forward, you have to refuel. You have to improve your mindset, develop your skillset, and increase your toolset.

Mindset is the most important component. But we will begin by defining and unpacking skillset and toolset.

Skillset
Your skillset is a range of abilities that has the potential to facilitate the

achievement of a goal or endeavor. Skills can generally fit within the following three categories[10]:

1. Cognitive
2. Socio-emotional
3. Technical

Cognitive skills are the range of abilities that facilitate learning, understanding, and information processing. Socio-emotional skills are the skills which enable effective interpersonal relationships and interactions. Examples of socio-emotional skills are emotional intelligence, communication, and teamwork. Technical skills are skills which facilitate the completion of a task or responsibility.

As you can imagine, these skills do not operate independently. Within any role or task, whether personal or professional, there are combinations of cognitive, socio-emotional, and technical skills that are necessary. It is therefore critical to assess and examine your level of skill in all three categories to identify where a skill gap may exist.

Once a skill gap is identified, development of that skill will be a part of your transformative journey. There are three keys to skill development[10]:

1. Content
2. Coaching
3. Continuous practice and improvement

The first key is content. To develop cognitive skills you must have access to quality information beyond which you already know. Information can be sourced from a wide variety of tools, people, and resources. The information must be credible for it to aid in cognitive skill development.

After consuming credible content, the understanding, context, and application of the information can be made most effective with a coach. A coach helps extend the content beyond its original emergence. You may hear new information at a conference, which opens your mind to additional possibilities. To apply the information you heard to your personal context, it can help to have a coach partner with you on the journey from information attainment to application to realized transformation.

The third key is continuous practice and improvement. There is a saying that "practice makes perfect." But in all honesty, practice perfects what you are practicing. So if you captured and are applying incorrect information, you are working towards perfecting something erroneous. Additionally, if you captured the correct information but interpreted it incorrectly, you would again be working towards perfecting something erroneous. Therefore, you must first ensure that the information you are applying is accurate. You must then ensure that your application of the information is fruitful. As you pursue and gain new skills, continue to practice and improve. This is the way to keep skills fresh and to continue to build upon the various levels of skills.

These three keys will enable you to build your skillset. But it takes all three keys. There is a saying that says, "Knowledge is learned. But skills are built."[11] You can learn new information. But the skills you need to apply the information must be built and developed. Skill building requires application, which is why the first key of content is not sufficient on its own. There must be application of what has been learned. Coaching can help guide the application. But it is through continuous practice and iterative improvements that skills are mastered.

As an example, if I am seeking to learn how to swim, I can read all the content in the world on swimming techniques. Getting a coach or trainer to help guide me in applying what I may have read regarding swimming is also helpful. But it is not until I actually get into the water to start to practice what I have learned that I will have the ability to master the skill of swimming. More advanced skills are created by building on top of foundational skills. There are varying levels of skills. As you master one level of skills, the next level is then available for you to obtain. Each level of skill will require more time, focus, and energy to build upon it.

Toolset
Your toolset is a collection of knowledge, resources, and systems that has the potential to extend your skillset and deepen the impact you can have on your surrounding environment. When it comes to tools, it is important to have awareness of and access to the appropriate tool and knowledge of how to use it. The keys to improved tools are:

1. Awareness
2. Access
3. Understanding

Activate Your Motivation to Move

Gaining access to knowledge, resources, and systems is essential to leveraging the benefits of a toolset. But you cannot access what you are not aware of. Therefore, it starts with awareness. We must be aware of the tools available that can help us grow and develop. Awareness is not always directly delivered to you. Sometimes you have to seek it yourself. Sometimes you have to stretch beyond what you have been given to reach the things you need that are higher than what others perceive you need.

One way to increase awareness is to immerse yourself in the areas related to your purpose and passion. Research those areas. Relentlessly pursue knowledge, resources, and systems that can assist you on your transformative journey. Pursue access to tools within the areas in which you seek to gain improvement.

Once you are aware of the tools and have access to them, you must then understand how to use them. There is a story about a young, strong, and experienced lumberjack who was hired at a local sawmill[29]. This sawmill was quite innovative and had the latest chainsaws available for their lumberjacks to use. Prior to this new position, the young lumberjack had only used the axe. He had great prowess with the use of the axe to chop down trees. Yet he had never used a chainsaw.

On his first day at work at this first-class sawmill, the young lumberjack was given a chainsaw to use to cut down the trees. He was not trained on the purpose of the tool or how to properly use it. The young lumberjack also failed to ask for guidance. Therefore, he found that after his first full day of work, he had only cut down three trees. His fellow co-workers had cut down twenty trees. Day after day, he found that this disparity in how many trees they cut down persisted. Finally, being concerned about the young lumberjack's lack of production, his manager shadowed him to observe his technique. The young lumberjack was attempting to use the chainsaw as an axe. He was beating the chainsaw against the tree instead of activating the power switch on the chainsaw and allowing the tool to do the hard work. This story reveals that having awareness of and access to the correct tool provides the potential to optimize productivity and results. However, without an understanding of how to use the tool, the results will not improve.

Notice that both skillsets and toolsets provide potential. It is mindset that transitions skillsets and toolsets from the state of potential to the state of power.

Mindset
Mindset refers to the thoughts, perceptions, emotions, and values that drive behavior. People tend to behave in a way that is consistent with how

Activate Your Motivation to Move

they see themselves. Reflect on the following questions regarding your mindset:

1. How do you see yourself?
2. Do you see the power you have today and the potential within your purpose?
3. Do you have the mindset you need to fully use the skillsets and toolsets you possess?
4. What is your mind set on? Is your mind set on the problems of the past or the possibilities of the future?
5. Is your mind set on your current place or the place to which you can be transported?

It is the mindset that makes the difference. Another model that reveals the importance of mindset is a revised version of the be-do-have model. There is a leadership model referenced by Zig Ziglar and Stephen Covey called the be-do-have model. The premise of this model is that in order to truly achieve a desired goal or vision, one must first determine the type of person or group they would need to **be** in order to **do** the things they need to do in order to **have** the things they wish to have[14].

However, I believe there is an additional component that proceeds this be-do-have model. The way I leverage this model is by adding the criticality of thought patterns. The model I employ is the **think**-be-do-have model. As the proverb states, "As a man thinketh, so is he." This proverb does not state "as a man has been told he is" or even "as a man actually is." The proverb centers on the fact that our thoughts have a powerful connection to what we become. It is impossible to think negatively and be positive. It is impossible to think selfishly and be selfless. Our thinking has an undeniable impact on our being. Therefore, to have the transportation that comes from transformation, we must think the way we need to **think** in order to **be** who we need to be, in order to **do** the things we need to do, and in order to **have** the transportation we seek to have. It starts with our minds.

As we examine our mindset, we must determine whether we are operating with a growth mindset or a fixed mindset when it comes to our journey of growth and development.

A growth mindset refers to the belief that the current state is not a static state and that improvement is possible. An individual with a growth mindset will view situations and circumstances with a comma or semicolon transition and not a period ending. They will see that this current situation is not the end of the journey. It is only a comma or semicolon that gives the opportunity for a new direction. Therefore, a transitional word will be coming, and the next part can be vastly different than the beginning.

Activate Your Motivation to Move

A transitional word such as "however" or "but" or "yet" or "nevertheless" or "conversely" may be around the corner. The sentence may read, "She had a tumultuous childhood; *however*, her gifts and talents could not be hidden." Or the sentence may say, "He was consistently overlooked, *yet* somehow his resume ended up in the right hands." A growth mindset consistently sees that a better situation is possible.

A fixed mindset is one that believes that conditions are unalterable and do not change over time. It is possible to have a growth mindset in some areas of your life and a fixed mindset in others. It is possible to have a growth mindset as it relates to the growth and development of others. But when considering your own growth trajectory, you may allow your challenges and mistakes to limit your ability to see that growth is also possible for you.

Activate Your Motivation to Move

There are certain spaces where a fixed mindset is appropriate. Certain decisions and principles will require an unwavering commitment to a position or stance. However, when it comes to the topic of this book, which is the transportation that results from transformative personal growth and development, a growth mindset is paramount. A growth mindset provides the fuel to move. It provides the belief that the transportation that will come as a result of this transformation is possible and purposeful.

Perspective
The primary driver of mindset is perspective. Perspective is the chosen point of view that drives one's understanding. Your perspective is your choice. This choice is one that can either push you towards a growth mindset or a fixed mindset. It can be the difference between your mind being an instrument of growth propelling you forward or an inhibiting force pushing you backwards.

Activate Your Motivation to Move

To mold our perspective, we can use the tool of reframing. As Henry David Thoreau once stated, "It's not what you look at that matters; it's what you see." Earlier in this chapter, we discussed how we see. But the way we frame something determines what we see. It is our perspective.

There are pictures that have been captured wherein multiple images can be seen. Multiple people can view these same pictures and may see different images. Here is one image as an example[39]:

Activate Your Motivation to Move

When initially viewing this image, what do you see? Some may see a young woman, while others may see an elderly woman. What some may view as the young woman's chin, others may see as the nose of an older woman. There may be situations in life where you view yourself as being too old or too young to take advantage of opportunities that may be presented to you. Yet someone else, a trustworthy purpose partner or someone in your corner or on your personal advisory board, may be able to point out a different perspective.

Here is another image[38]:

What do you see in this image? Do you see a duck or a rabbit? Depending on which direction you assume this animal is facing will determine what you see. At times, we can find ourselves facing backwards as we focus on our past. We could be focused on our past mistakes and accept those mistakes as limitations. Or we could be focused on our past accomplishments and accept those accomplishments as our peak, determining we have nowhere else to grow. But again, we have the ability to change our perspective.

When facing change, we can have the perspective that this is a change that is happening *to* me. Yet this perspective strips us of our autonomy and can lead to a fixed mindset. Or we can shift our perspective by reframing it from something that is happening *to* me to something that is happening *for* me. We can view this same situation of change and say, "What can I gain from this change? Can I gain strength or resilience from this? Is this an opportunity for me to demonstrate that I can grow and excel even in the midst of uncertainty?" Change is inevitable, but growth and progress are not. Growth and progress require intention.

As another example, the Chinese word for crisis is Wei Ji 危机. When broken down into its two components, wei (危) means danger, while ji (机) means opportunity[5]. When in crisis, we have the ability to see the danger side of the situation, or we can see the opportunity within the situation. What we see will determine what we think and do. The opportunity side is not always easy to see. But it exists. There are always two sides. It may take someone else to point it out to us. It may take time for the tears to dry so that we can see the other side. It may take time for the dust to clear so that we can see the other side. It may take climbing the mountain in order for us to see the other side. But the other side is there. Keep pushing. Keep moving forward. Keep climbing.

When facing rejection, we can choose to have the perspective that this is rejection. Yet that perspective can lead us down a destructive path of negative thinking. On the other hand, we can shift our perspective by reframing it to see that this is a redirection to properly position us for success. We have to shift our "what if" thinking into "even

Activate Your Motivation to Move

if" thinking. Our "what if" thinking is our negative thinking and framing. But our "even if" thinking is a determined mindset. This mindset yields the belief that even if there are challenges, the challenges do not have the power to stop us. We would have to choose to stop. Since perspective is a choice, we can choose to have the mindset and perspective that will allow us to overcome and not succumb.

I was watching an episode of the Justice League Unlimited cartoon with my son. In the episode, Superman was facing a vicious opponent named Darkseid[28]. Darkseid was ruthless, strong, and unmerciful. Superman's response to this overwhelming challenge caught my attention. Superman said, "What we have here is a rare opportunity for me to cut loose and show you just how powerful I really am!" How do you respond to challenging situations? Do you view them as overwhelming obstacles that can defeat you or stop your progress?

Or do you see challenging situations as rare opportunities to cut loose and show how powerful you truly are?

In the movie Frozen, the main character Elsa showed her power early on in her life. Others perceived her power as too great. She was then told, "Conceal it. Don't feel it. Don't let it show." But our power and our strength are necessary. As we learn to focus and leverage our power and strength, we will discover mental fortitude that will enable us to endure and persevere as we continuously grow and transform. Hiding our power and strength does not strengthen our character or our will. It actually diminishes our character and our will. It is our character and our will that allow us to continue moving through the transportation of transformation.

Be Ready for the Ride
As a child, I remember an instance where I went to an amusement park

with my friends. We got in line to ride a roller coaster, and we were all teasing each other and claiming how brave we were. I was quick to say, "I'm not going to scream when I get on this ride," only to get towards the front of the line and see the ridiculous, discriminatory sign that said you have to be a certain height to ride the ride. I was really upset. I went home and told my dad about what happened. My dad responded in his typical way, as he asked me to research why the sign was there. As I researched it, I learned that the purpose of the sign is to ensure that those who ride the ride have grown enough that they are able to withstand the force of the ride. Many people want to get on the ride of the next level. But there is a force that comes with the ride. And we need to grow enough so that we can withstand the peaks and valleys and the twists and turns of the ride.

Coming back a few years later, I was able to ride and conquer the roller coaster. I had to grow into the ability to endure the ride. I had to gain confidence that I was strapped in safely and securely. I had to have assurance that I was properly positioned for the journey. Some may get on the ride of the next level prematurely. They may not have grown and developed enough to withstand the force. So as they progress through the ride, they keep their eyes closed tightly the whole time, or they spend the entire ride screaming and crying, only to get off the ride feeling sick and wanting to go home.

Many people go through their current role or position in life this way. Many people are placed in situations, roles, or positions in life that they are not quite prepared for. They have not experienced the necessary growth and transformation they need to be secure in the position, situation, or circumstance they are in. However, when you continually grow, develop, and transform; you are ready for your next level when it is revealed. You will then enjoy the ride. You will get off the ride looking at those around you and saying "That was fun! Now, what's next?"

There is tremendous power in the ability to grow and transform. For it is far more powerful and rewarding to grow into a new position or situation than to be placed in one in which we are not yet ready.

As stated in the previous chapter, this world needs you. This world needs the transformed version of you - the best version of you. That is the version that optimizes your gifts, talents, and character. As Socrates once stated, "Let him that would move the world, first move himself." It is time to move. It's time to leverage the transportation of transformation.

3

Prepare for Your Journey

As a review, the four sets of key principles of movement are:

1. Power & Strength
2. Speed & Momentum
3. Balance & Flexibility
4. Endurance & Perseverance

We have covered the first two sets of principles. The third set of principles will be the focus of this chapter. As we embark upon the transportation of transformation, it is critical that we maintain balance and flexibility to stay on course.

Challenges and obstacles will come. We are committed to the outcome, not the predefined journey to get there. Therefore, we must remain aware of the various challenges and obstacles we encounter and create necessary mitigation plans to ensure we maintain our focus on the desired outcome – our transformation.

Identifying the Next Destination
Before covering the importance of balance and flexibility, we will first cover the topic of identifying our next destination. As we go through the process of identifying our next destination in the pursuit of our purposed potential, we will leverage a three-step process by which we will:

1. Reflect
2. Examine
3. Assess

Self-reflection brings about awareness. But it is the assessment and examination phase that will lead to an

Prepare for Your Journey

understanding of the opportunity to improve and transform. Imagine you have eaten a very delicious yet somewhat messy dessert. You can feel that you have some evidence of the dessert on your face. You can tell by the reactions of others around you that something is wrong. Taking the time to look in the mirror will not fix the problem. Looking in the mirror can provide you with awareness and confirmation that there is indeed something on your face that needs to be addressed. However, in order for this to be true, you have to not only look in the mirror, but you have to be willing to see the full image. If you look in the mirror but refuse to look at your face, you may miss the remnants of the dessert that are left on your cheek.

Awareness of an issue can be generated by noticing the reactions of others. However, it is not until you see and accept it yourself that it can be addressed and resolved. When we reflect on our journey, we must be willing to look at our full story. We often accept our blind spots and choose to limit our vision. This keeps us from addressing our issues and thereby causes us to condone and accept the blemishes we have. We all have mountaintops and valleys in our life's journey. But every mountaintop and every valley have a purpose. We must see it all. We do not have to settle for a life with persistent blemishes. We do not have to stop the process once we identify an area we want to transform. We can see it, examine it, assess it, and transform it.

Reflect
As we previously covered, by reflecting on our lives, we can identify themes that can help us point to our purpose. The comprehensive self-reflection also reveals persistent areas we wish to strengthen or transform. What areas of your life require focus and attention? Identifying these areas will help us when we determine our next

destination, or the characteristics we seek to gain in the next version of ourselves.

Reflecting on our journey and viewing it in completion is only step one. Once we are aware of the areas requiring development, the next step is to examine and assess them.

Examine
The Greek philosopher Socrates stressed the importance of continuously examining life. In his work, Apology, Socrates speaks of the importance of living an "examined life." In his writing, Socrates highlights the importance of introspection, understanding, and living with purpose[22]. When examination of one's self and one's surroundings is lacking, opportunities are missed, purpose is unfulfilled, and meaning remains undiscovered. It is similar to floating in the ocean without a sail or an anchor. You would find yourself drifting

wherever the wind decided to carry the vessel, with no preparation for potential storms.

The other option is to live an examined life. This examined life is one in which we develop an understanding of who we are, why we exist, and what our purpose is. The examined life is also one where we have an understanding of how we can optimize our current state and surroundings to propel us into our progression towards our purposed potential. When living an examined life, we can gain an understanding of our current nature, strengths, weaknesses, and direction. This understanding can help us as we approach the assessment stage. The assessment stage is where we can determine if there is a need to adjust our sails, set our anchor, raise our anchor, or explore uncharted territories.

In 2008, there was a hurricane that destroyed a neighborhood in Gilchrist, Texas, that had about 200 homes[24].

Prepare for Your Journey

Every home in that area was completely wiped out, except for one. What was different about this one house that remained? This particular house had been destroyed three years earlier by Hurricane Rita. After that devastating loss from Hurricane Rita, the owners decided to make a change. They invested time, energy, and money to find and leverage the skills of a master builder who specialized in the design and construction of structures that were strong enough to withstand these storms.

The homeowners could have simply rebuilt their home exactly as it was, ignoring the outcome they had recently experienced. They could have chosen to only think or talk about what they could do differently. But instead, they decided to make the choice and the investment to take action and make a change. This choice paid off when, three years later, they found themselves facing yet another storm. This time, they were prepared. They were built differently. They were confident in their foundation since they had fortified it. They upgraded their materials. They were now protected and prepared.

Similarly, it is important to leverage the storms we have endured to make a positive difference. Do not let the opportunity to learn pass by you. There is a lesson and a purpose in every storm. Do not waste the storm. Do not waste the pain. I truly believe that every storm, trial, or challenge should be profitable, meaning that we should get more out of it than what it takes from us. We should gain something on the other side of the pain. We must adapt to secure our readiness for the next battle or storm that we may face. We must transform and rebuild our structure to ensure we can persevere through the next challenge. To effectively and fruitfully transform, we must examine and assess our current state and location.

Prepare for Your Journey

There is a difference between examining and assessing. The word examine means to deeply study something in detail to determine its nature, form, and current condition. The key to examination is understanding. By examining ourselves, we are studying our current condition and state without assigning judgment. We are simply identifying our starting point. Examination either unveils new information or affirms known facts. In contrast, the word assess means to evaluate or assign a value to something.

Assess
An assessment is an evaluation. It goes a step further than the examination, which provides an understanding of an area requiring focus and improvement. The examination phase provides the "what" that needs transformation. The assessment phase reveals "where" the transformation needs to occur and feeds into "how" the transformation can transpire.

Prepare for Your Journey

One example of the assessment phase is the soil health assessment process. The process to assess soil health is intended to determine the soil's current ability to perform its expected functions and evaluate the manner in which those functions are preserved and developed for future use. There is a comprehensive process to evaluate soil health that includes a number of indicators and measurements.

Similarly, when we assess the soil in which we are currently planted, we can also use indicators and measurements as evaluation criteria. We can assess our internal current state. We can also assess the environment around us, which includes the nouns we interact with – people, places, and things. First, we can determine how effective our current state is by evaluating our ability to fulfill and realize our potential.

As improvements are made and we reach higher levels of improvement, we must maintain and sustain the

Prepare for Your Journey

improvement. How are we preserving improvements so that one level of improvement can fuel our next level of transformation? We do not want to lose ground. So as we grow and develop, we must have strategies and routines to ensure that what we gain is sustained and becomes part of our daily routines and habits. It should become part of who we are.

With that in mind, it is critical to define what we seek to transform into as a result of the next phase of our journey. Our current state will have imperfections. It is easy to grow comfortable and complacent, accepting the imperfections. Instead of falling into complacency, we can define the characteristics that are within the next version of ourselves that we seek to gain through the transformation.

Our next destination can be found in our purpose and potential. Purpose and potential are harvested from the seeds of faith and exposure. Your faith in your ability to reach the next version of yourself comes from the memory of your evolutionary journey thus far. The definition of possible is relative. It is often dependent on what one has experienced and seen.

If you think back ten years ago, five years ago, or even one year ago, what has changed in you? In what areas have you grown? What has been awakened or strengthened within you? Your ability to grow in these time periods is proof of the fact that you can progress and get better. Better is possible. You can believe in your ability to grow because you have grown. You can believe in your ability to develop because you have developed.

Exposure creates appetites. Imagine your favorite food item. Think about how delicious it is. Had you never been exposed to it, never smelled it, never seen it, or never tasted it, you would never want it or crave it. Your appetite was created because you were exposed

Prepare for Your Journey

to something better than what you had known. Our current experience can be mistakenly labeled as the best or most optimal, until we experience better. When being exposed to something better, it should not create envy; it should create inspiration and appetite. It should become a catalytic determination that allows you to believe, "I am bound for better." This increased appetite will enable you to be purposeful about your journey of transformation. It will help you define the path you seek to take.

All caterpillars that transform do not become butterflies. Some caterpillars become butterflies. But other caterpillars become moths. Just as superheroes and villains both have exceptional abilities. As they develop, what they become is greatly influenced by their mindsets. Superheroes and villains both have extraordinary skillsets and toolsets. But the difference is in their mindsets. Villains generally have their minds set on selfish agendas.

Prepare for Your Journey

Whereas their superhero counterparts have their minds set on serving and helping others who cannot help themselves. The difference in their mindset impacts what they choose to do with their power. Their power is employed in alignment with their mindset.

Explore the following questions to frame your next stage of development:

1. What do you believe you should be doing with your power on this next evolutionary journey?
2. Who do you hope to serve and contribute to during this next leg of your life's journey?
3. What type of appetite have exposure and faith created in you?
4. What do you hope to *gain* during this leg of your life's journey?
5. What do you hope to *give* during this leg of your life's journey?

Prepare for Your Journey

This then becomes the purpose of your next destination. This is where you are headed. This is your goal. The definition of the word goal is the destination towards which effort is focused. From this definition, we can derive some key benefits that result from defining a targeted destination.

The first benefit is purpose. When you are aware of your intended destination, you do not live life aimlessly. You can prepare with purpose. You can serve with purpose. You can move with purpose. This purposeful destination becomes where your time, energy, and effort can be focused.

Once the purpose of your targeted destination is defined, it unlocks the other two benefits: direction and focus. When you do not have a destination or goal in mind, someone else will craft a goal or place for you that benefits them. As Alice Walker clarified, "The most common way people give up their power is by thinking they don't have any." We have the power to choose the direction of our lives. Do not give this power away.

Once the destination is identified, we now have the ability to set an intentional course that will lead us in the direction of our destination. A defined destination also provides us with a vision that is forward-facing. We do not have to live life looking backwards when we have a destination that we are progressing towards.

This then brings us to the third benefit, which is focus. As mentioned earlier, the definition of focus is selective attention. Our attention has value. It is currency, and it should earn a return. That which you pay attention to, you will develop. If you are paying attention to drama and distractions, you are cultivating and developing that drama and those distractions. Having a destination on which we can focus enables us to distinguish purposeful and fruitful efforts from distractions. It enables us to say "no" to distractions so that we are available to say "yes" to the things that will allow us to reach our destination.

Charting the Path
Now that we know where we are headed, we can plan a path to get there. The plan we create is the initial plan, which provides a sense of direction and purposeful steps. However, we must remain flexible within our plan.

It is great to decide on a destination. However, without a plan to reach that destination, it will seem out of reach. As James Clear explains, "You do not rise to the level of your goals. You fall to the level of your systems. Your goal is your desired outcome. But your system is the collection of daily habits that will get you there[16]."

Mark Victor Hansen created an acronym for system that I have found to be true.

Prepare for Your Journey

Having a system:

- **S**aves
- **Y**ou
- **S**tress
- **T**ime
- **E**nergy, and
- **M**oney

Your system will include necessary choices, mindsets, and actions that will help you reach your desired destination. This system will require you to proactively think through the conceivable obstacles or challenges you might encounter along your journey to reach the targeted destination. You can then develop mitigation plans to include as part of your system. Ultimately, the system is comprised of your daily habits and routines that will pave the path to your purposed potential. The paving of this path and the development of systematic habits and routines begin in the mind.

Prepare for Your Journey

I have always had a love for architecture. Architecture is the practice of purposefully and effectively planning and designing structures. So when I first heard the term psychitecture, I was intrigued. Pychitecture is the practice of purposefully and effectively designing experiences that can reset various patterns within the mind that drive our instinctive thoughts, words, and actions[30]. This theory considers the fact that our brains are designed to operate based on patterns. The patterns of our experiences create expectations that our brains respond to in thought, words, or actions. As we recognize that we need a change in our instinctive thoughts, words, or actions, we do not have to settle for suboptimal living. We can create a series of experiences to create new patterns to retrain our minds and result in the transformation necessary for our transportation to our next developmental destination.

Neuroscience supports this as well. Neuroplasticity is the term used to

Prepare for Your Journey

describe the ability of the brain to alter and reset patterns through learning and conditioning[33]. Our brains are consistently learning and adding new experiences to their programming. Whether intentional or unintentional, you are creating patterns and sowing seeds that will one day reap a harvest. You are sowing seeds of experiences or interpretations that will reap the harvest of thoughts, words, actions, and habits.

Psychitecture is centered on leveraging the capability of neuroplasticity to impact three areas: cognitive, emotional, and behavioral[30]. The cognitive area refers to our convictions, interpretations, biases, prudence, and reflection. The emotional component is where our responses to feelings such as pain, stress, and temptations reside. The behavioral area refers to our routines, habits, and actions.

As we prepare for this journey of transformation, we will need balance and flexibility to deal with the various changes that will come. We can create various cognitive, emotional, and behavioral plans to help us circumvent avoidable roadblocks. It is difficult to develop a plan while you are traveling. So we must prepare for war in the time of peace. We must create mitigation plans in the event we encounter certain triggers to ensure we can maintain our focus and direction.

The transportation of transformation is not a smooth path without challenges or obstacles. Therefore, before embarking on the journey, we must create plans to ensure that we are balanced and flexible to enable us to persevere through challenges.

Cognitive Balance and Flexibility
One component of a plan to avoid cognitive roadblocks is to adopt the posture of a student. This is my favorite posture. It is a posture in which you are continually seeking and are ready to learn. In this posture, you prioritize the attainment of new

information and experiences above the comfort of your existing level of knowledge. You do not discount or degrade your existing knowledge, but you do not limit yourself to your current state. You are open to hearing new information that can be explored and examined. The posture of a student creates doors and windows instead of walls. Statements build walls, while questions create doors and windows. Accordingly, in this posture, instead of making statements affirming your current knowledge, strategic questions are used to explore other ideas and deepen your knowledge base.

When you approach situations, conversations, and interactions in this posture, it enables you to circumvent many mental hurdles. One hurdle you will circumvent is bias. A bias is an inclination to favor one thing over another. Biases may lead to a distortion of judgment[26]. There are many types and reasons for biases.

One type of bias is confirmation bias. Those operating with a confirmation bias will be inclined to favor experiences or information that align with their existing knowledge or ideas[26]. Approaching events and interactions with the posture of a student protects us against this bias. In the student's posture, we become excited about the possibility of expanding our bank of knowledge. In this posture, we are seeking expansion of knowledge, not affirmation of what we already know. We prioritize expansion over predetermination.

To provide another example of how a student's posture combats bias, we will explore a second type of bias. Anchoring bias is a bias that reflects one's propensity to latch onto and be driven by the first insight received. Operating with this bias causes people to sacrifice the opportunity to grow and develop, as they will ignore subsequent data once they have anchored their decisions and conclusions to the first piece of data presented. The student's posture combats this bias by leveraging the windows and doors of the posture to remain open to exploration of new territories of learning. New information can be evaluated to determine how it compares or conflicts with the first piece of data presented. Through exploration, examination, and assessment, the validity, relevance, and applicability of new information can be confirmed.

Additionally, when creating a plan to mitigate potential blocks in our cognitive development, we must go beyond just examining our singular thoughts and biases. We must also evaluate the patterns of experiences and behaviors that lead to the thoughts that enter our minds. If we recognize that we react to a specific triggering event or interaction with a negative thought, we must evaluate how that thought came to be.

Prepare for Your Journey

To truly plan for potential blocks that may occur, we have to go deeper than a singular thought. It is the thought patterns that we need to examine and assess. We should explore the patterns of experiences that led to that thought. Why did hearing the answer "no" lead to defeating thoughts? Were there a series of experiences that you had or that you heard of in which the answer "no" led to devastating consequences? It is the series of events that laid the pavers along the path that leads to the thought. More specifically, it is our interpretation of each experience that results in the paver placed on the path. Therefore, we must use the power of reframing the past experiences that we recognize as pavers along our thought process and path. We may not control what thoughts pop into our minds, but we do control how long they remain there.

For example, if we apply for a job and do not get it, what thoughts come to mind? Are they thoughts of rejection or thoughts of redirection and protection? The following thoughts may pop into our minds: "I am not good enough for that door to open for me to get that job. I must not be smart enough." If those defeating thoughts pop into our mind, we can reframe the situation and shift the thought to say, "It is not that I am not good enough for that door to open. But this simply means that this is not my door. This is not the role I am to occupy in this season. There is a more appropriate role for me." Reframing and rewriting the narrative of our experiences can mitigate the negative thought patterns that we recognize we possess.

Emotional Balance and Flexibility
Many luxury hotel chains leverage the use of access cards for the elevators that travel from floor to floor. Certain floors are only accessible to those who possess the correct access cards. We should operate the same way with our lives. Just because someone pushes a button for a certain floor does not

Prepare for Your Journey

automatically mean that you have to meet them at the floor for which they pushed the button.

You should not allow everyone you encounter to have cards with the same level of access to you. Someone's access to you does not depend on what they want; it depends on what you allow. It is pertinent to identify your triggers. What pushes your buttons? Once you identify your triggers, you can create plans to effectively recognize and manage them. This will enable you to maintain focus on your journey of transformation.

To create a plan to mitigate emotional roadblocks, we will first cover emotional intelligence. Emotional intelligence is the ability to recognize and manage one's emotions and those of others around them to optimally impact the emotional environment[34]. Emotional intelligence is primarily about awareness and management of two emotional perspectives: your own and the perspective of others. But as with any type of intelligence, it is only valuable in its application. The transportation of transformation can be a bumpy ride with challenges and obstacles. Applying emotional intelligence will make it possible to maintain balance throughout the transportation of transformation.

One component of an emotional mitigation plan is to regularly reflect, assess, and examine your emotions. The emotions you feel are real. However, they may not always be based on accurate understanding. Your emotions are the result of your thinking and interpretation. If something happens, it is how you interpret what took place that will depict your emotions towards it. Yet, at times, our interpretation or perspective may not be based on accurate or complete information. That would then lead us to have unsubstantiated emotions.

For example, one day when I was a child, I was walking in the yard as my dad was on the deck cooking on the grill. I saw a bucket, and as I leaned over to look in it, I saw what looked to be a snake. I was immediately filled with fear. I screamed and took off, running into the house. My dad came inside and asked me what happened. I told him what I saw, and he told me to come back outside. He told me to look into the bucket. He held my hand, and as I looked in the bucket, I realized that it was not a snake. It was simply a wet towel rolled up. The fear I felt was real. The fear resulted in an adrenaline boost that gave me the power to run faster than I had ever run before. But it was based on inaccurate information. Had I known that it was a wet towel, my thoughts and resulting emotions and actions would have been different. Therefore, before acting, we must assess and examine the emotions to ensure they are anchored to real information, accurate interpretations, and appropriate perspectives.

Prepare for Your Journey

Another component of the emotional mitigation plan is to identify your emotional triggers. An emotional trigger refers to an event or occurrence that initiates instinctive responses leading to a specific reaction. Before embarking on the journey of transformation, it is helpful to identify and examine our current emotional triggers. This will enable us to develop mitigation plans ahead of the time when we need them. Once again, it is always better to prepare for war in a time of peace. While in the heat of the battle, it is extremely difficult to develop an effective and comprehensive strategy to deal with the current attacks. The most effective strategies are developed before the battle begins.

As an example, I am driven by impact. I know I was created to make an impact. So, early in my career, I had to learn to manage situations where my contribution, impact, or value was dismissed, unappreciated, or attributed to someone else. These situations triggered the emotions of frustration, disappointment, and self-doubt. Those emotions resulted in actions such as shutting down and disengaging. Those reactions hinder progress towards my purpose. Those reactions would destroy the personal brand I had worked to build. I was not willing to accept the hindrance. I was not willing to stop my progress. Therefore, I had to create a mitigation plan.

I had to reflect on the various situations in which I had experienced this. I had to understand the context of each situation. I had to examine and assess the various perspectives and the origins of my thoughts and emotions. I then had to examine and assess my instinctive actions to determine what needed to change.

I determined that what I needed to change was how I defined and verified my impact. I had unintentionally placed the validation of my value in the hands of others. The change I made was to strengthen the confidence I had in my own value and in the contribution and impact I knew I was capable of making. I had to change how I measured and validated my impact and the difference I make. I could not solely leave it in the hands of others. I had to be able to triangulate the feedback from others with objective, tangible measurements as well.

There were times when others ignored my value, contribution, and impact. There were also times when people praised my value, contribution, and impact when I knew I had not done my best. Thus, I had to change my measurement and validation to include multiple streams of input and data.

When assessing and examining the situations I reflected on, I realized that there were two categories of situations. The first category was situations where what I offered was not of the value I thought it had. I overestimated and miscalculated the value of my contribution. The second category was situations where others either could not or chose not to see the actual value in what I contributed to the space.

In those situations where I miscalculated the value of my contribution, I realized that I could have approached those situations differently. I learned the power of leveraging strategic questions to gain the necessary feedback to do an effective needs analysis. This would enable me to appropriately determine the depth and breadth of impact that are necessary. Strategic questions also provided me with the opportunity to incorporate additional perspectives into my contribution. I was able to identify additional mindsets, skills, and tools I could leverage to strengthen what I contribute. There is always room to add, multiply, and exponentially increase the positive impact and contribution you make.

Prepare for Your Journey

The feedback and response to what has happened can inform the change and transformation of what you will do moving forward. Feed-back, translated to feed-forward, facilitates this increase. Constructive feedback, responses, and reactions are data points that you can either allow to break you, or you can use them to build a better version of yourself.

People do not always relay feedback in the most respectful and kind ways. Instead of throwing respectful, constructive, and helpful streams of information, people can throw bricks of hurtful and degrading remarks. But once the brick is thrown my way, it is mine to use however I choose. I choose to use it to build and fortify my foundation. So regardless of how it is packaged, I will extract something from the feedback I receive to strengthen myself for the path forward. Those who voiced unkind things may have intended to harm me, but I chose to use them to help me instead. Now, in my career and in my personal life, I seek out feedback. I yearn for ways to improve and higher levels of excellence to strive for.

In those situations where others could not accurately see value in what I contributed, I had to review the manner in which I presented my contribution. There may be areas that I could develop in terms of my communication and presentation of the value that I have to offer. In the first chapter, we reviewed the importance of knowing your present power. But then it is important to gain the skills to communicate the strength and power you possess. Then we covered leveraging that present power to propel us towards our purposed potential. We should continuously seek development in our communication and presentation of the strength and power we possess and will leverage. This is an example of where that skill is helpful.

In those situations where others refused to see the actual value in what I contributed to the space, I had to learn to separate others' responsibility and accountability from my responsibility and accountability. My mitigation plan around this component of the trigger was to accurately identify my accountability and responsibility. There is a difference between responsibility and accountability[14]. Responsibility is tied to a specific task or action. Accountability is the ownership over the overall outcome and results[14]. For example, let's say I am accountable for the success of a project. The project must meet specific goals within a specific timeline. I will assign various responsibilities throughout the team to complete specific tasks within the project. If someone fails to fulfill their responsibilities to complete a task, I am still accountable for the success of the project. Therefore, I must be able to manage the work and mitigate the issues to ensure the overall project I am accountable for is sustained. I am accountable for my brand and my identity. I am responsible for the integrity, character, effort, courage, commitment, preparation, and performance that culminate in my brand and identity. However, I am not responsible for other people's biases, choices, thoughts, or behaviors. I can influence and have an impact through the brand and the image that I project. However, I cannot take accountability for whether others receive me or what I have to offer.

I love to cook. But just because I cook a delicious meal does not mean that it will appease every palate. Some may not be able to properly digest what I have prepared. Some may have allergies or digestive problems that may keep them from tasting what I have prepared. It is my goal to prepare the best meal I can with the ingredients, recipes, and tools that I have at my disposal. I am accountable for preparing and serving the dish. Those who are meant to eat the meal I prepare and gain strength from it will. This is the perspective we must take when it comes to the opinions and rejections of others. Take the positive insights you can from comments, but do not allow the negativity to stop your transportation of transformation.

These mitigation plans have empowered me to sustain my focus and maintain my progress on the path to purposed potential, even when triggering situations occur. Once we identify the current triggers we have, we must create mitigation plans to manage each trigger.

Behavioral Balance and Flexibility
As stated earlier, your system is comprised of your daily habits and routines. These habits and routines are learned and formed over time. However, they can be unlearned and changed when transformation is necessary.

Prepare for Your Journey

In his book, *The Power of Habit*, Charles Duhigg provides three key components of habits[15]:

1. Cue
2. Routine
3. Reward

The cue triggers an action. This action comes in the form of a routine that results in a consequence or a reward.

In the book *Atomic Habits*, James Clear conveys stages for building habits. The stages he reveals are similar to those provided by Charles Duhigg. In James Clear's stages, he breaks down the routine into two parts. In response to the cue, James Clear describes a craving stage and a response stage. These two stages comprise the routine stage in Charles Duhigg's model.

The craving stage provides the motive to act. The motive is often the desired receipt of the reward you expect as a result of the action you will take. The strength of this craving will determine whether there is a response to it. The response then generates the corresponding reward or consequence. James Clear's four-stage model of habit formation[16] is as follows:

1. Cue
2. Craving
3. Response
4. Reward

Our habits have the ability to shape our destiny. The good thing is that we can change our habits to shift the course of our destiny. As we identify the areas of our lives where transformation is needed, we can pinpoint the specific result in which we are not satisfied. Once we identify the result that needs to change, we can go back to the response, craving, and cue that led to the resulting consequence.

It is in the examination and assessment phases that we truly dive into our results to identify patterns of thinking or routines of actions that are impacting our behaviors. As an example, at one point in my career, I noticed that I was overwhelmed at work. There were meetings in which I showed up unprepared. Personally, I take pride in my preparation. So showing up to meetings unprepared is not an acceptable result. In recognizing this as an area I sought to improve, let's first break down the habit into its components. This will allow us to create a new habit and routine.

The cue is the recognition that I was not prepared. I did not have the time to review the materials ahead of the meeting. Therefore, I was not prepared with questions, additional information, or details. I generally like to show up to meetings with lists of unanswered questions and unquestioned answers. Addressing the unanswered questions will provide clarity. Raising the unquestioned answers often expands the discussion to include additional perspectives and to challenge biases.

Prepare for Your Journey

This generally leads to a more comprehensive and optimal result.

The craving was the confidence, clarity, and direction that I know I can bring to and receive from meetings. The response to that craving when I am unprepared may be to disengage. If I cannot show up prepared, I would prefer to not show up at all. The reward, or in this case, consequence to disengaging of damaging. It would appear that I did not know the answers I should know. It would appear that I am not interested in the topic. Therefore, the response needs to change.

The cue exists for a reason. The craving is a healthy craving. Therefore, it is the response that needs to change. I need to put in the work that would result in the ability to provide the confidence, clarity, and direction that I can bring.

To change a habit or routine, you can replace it with a routine that yields the results you are seeking. Let's create a new routine.

As you seek to establish a new habit, it is helpful to identify your approach to routines. Gretchen Rubin provides four tendencies related to routines[17]:

1. Upholder
2. Obliger
3. Questioner
4. Rebel

The upholder seeks to meet both internal and external expectations. Therefore, routines that have clear expectations work well for this personality. The obliger is willing to sacrifice internal promises and expectations for external satisfaction. For the obliger, routines wherein others are dependent on or expecting results will be more easily sustained. A system of accountability is helpful for the obliger tendency. The questioner prioritizes internal expectations above external expectations. The routines that are maintained by the questioner are those that align with the questioner's value, purpose, and intended results. Understanding the "why" is essential to the questioner. The rebel, on the other hand, will resist expectations, whether they be internal or external. The rebels thrive in routines where they have autonomy[17].

I recognize that my tendency toward routines is situational. However, I am most naturally a questioner. Since I am extremely purpose-driven, I seek to understand the purpose of my actions. When the purpose is strong enough, the sacrifice to obtain it becomes negligible. For this example, the "why" is to show up prepared for meetings and affirm my brand rather than distract from it. I would be able to maximize my impact. For me, this is a strong motive and reason. Therefore, I am more than willing to sacrifice to establish a new routine.

Prepare for Your Journey

I can adjust my routine to intentionally make time to prepare. Friday is the day of the week where I generally have significant time that is not spent in meetings. I can devote time each Friday to reviewing my meeting schedule and topics for the upcoming weeks. To reduce the friction in this new routine, I choose to document my upcoming schedule each Friday and will take notes on each meeting to properly prepare. This will enable me to review the scheduled meetings without having to search through my calendar or through various documents. I can consolidate it into one document. Additionally, I incorporated a daily change. I am a morning person. I have the most energy in the mornings. Therefore, I can also set my alarm clock earlier each weekday to have dedicated time to finalize my preparation for the meetings of the day. This adjustment is a true adjustment I made almost a decade ago, and it changed my approach to meetings and enabled me to be much more prepared and impactful.

In each of our lives, we will face challenges and new opportunities. Each new challenge and each new opportunity require a new approach, routine, and habits to be successful.

High Jump
In track and field, one event I competed in was the high jump. Generally, the girls that competed in the high jump event were quite tall. Although I am many things, being tall is not one of them. Initially, my own teammates questioned my abilities. They were teasing me because what I looked like did not match what they expected. My coach knew I could jump, which is why he had asked me to try out for the team. So as I saw him walking over to us, I expected that all the questioning, doubting, and insulting would be over.

Prepare for Your Journey

The coach looked at my teammates and said, "Instead of y'all picking on her, why don't we test her to see what she can do?"

That was not what I considered to be supportive leadership. I wanted him to step in and give them a message of what it means to be a team. I wanted him to tell them that they needed to be supportive and encouraging. But instead, he offered a stage for me to prove what I could do. I did not see it at the time, but somehow he knew that my actions would speak louder than his words ever could. So although it was not fair, I took the opportunity. They set the bar at four feet. I did my approach, and I cleared it. They raised the bar, and I cleared it again. They raised it again and again until it reached the highest height that had been jumped by anyone on the team. I cleared it each time. There were three lessons that I gained from this experience that I carry with me.

Prepare for Your Journey

The first lesson is that although I know what I can do, that does not mean others will automatically believe what I can do. We have to have the audacity to believe in our abilities to achieve our goals, even when others may doubt us. We have to believe when others tell us what they think we are unable to do or achieve. We have to have the courage and grit to hold onto the knowledge of who we are and the power we possess.

The second lesson is the importance of capitalizing on opportunities to show what I am able to do. Opportunity is not always convenient. We must remain in a state of readiness. We have to continue to develop our weaknesses and optimize our strengths. This will ensure that when the right opportunity arises, you can boldly step into any space and unleash the power that is inside of you.

The third lesson I learned was that no matter how high the bar is raised, I can meet the goal. Each time the bar was raised, the reason I was able to clear it was that I adapted my approach. As the bar got higher, I had to change my pacing and my momentum. When the bar was at its highest height, I had to add more steps to my approach. Your approach is your system. It is the daily routines and habits you exercise. Each time the bar is raised, each time a new goal is set, or each time a new level is reached, your system and approach will need to change.

You may encounter significant challenges and obstacles during the journey to reach your goal. The existence of challenges and obstacles does not mean that you cannot overcome and achieve them. In fact, it means that when you do accomplish that goal, you will have gained additional strength and power in the process that will give you the ability, strength, grit, and determination to stand when others cannot. When you have had to work for it, shed tears for it, fight for it, get up early for it, and

Prepare for Your Journey

stay up late for it, you are not going to give up so easily. You will not give up just because the journey gets hard. You will not quit just because a hurdle arises. You will leverage your balance and flexibility to overcome. No matter how high the bar is raised, you can and will clear it.

4

Achieve Your Purposed Potential

Anchoring back to the four sets of key principles of movement:

1. Power & Strength
2. Speed & Momentum
3. Balance & Flexibility
4. Endurance & Perseverance

In this chapter, we will focus on endurance and perseverance. We have limited control over the things we will encounter during the transportation of transformation. So our focus should not be on control. Our focus should be on the courage to endure and persevere.

Endurance is the ability to exercise stamina to withstand a prolonged and challenging process or situation without giving up. Perseverance goes a step further than withstanding. Perseverance refers to the tenacity to exert the energy and effort required to overcome and achieve a goal despite difficulty, challenges, or opposition.

The only way to build stamina and endurance is to run a greater distance or function at a higher level than previously accomplished. This is the purpose of the transformation - to be transported beyond where you are today.

In his book *Endure*, Alex Hutchinson presents many findings related to the optimization of performance. As outlined within the book, the mind has a powerful role in a key driver of performance: endurance and perseverance[18]. It is the mind that instructs the body on when to start, accelerate, decelerate, and stop. The central governor model refers to the regulatory nature of the brain. The model posits that the brain serves as both the command post and the safety shutdown valve for the body[19]. The mind communicates to the body when it is approaching or has reached its limit. This is the reason mindset is so critical to our transportation of transformation. Our mind is a key component of our endurance and perseverance.

As we travel through the transportation of transformation, we will experience challenges and obstacles. This is where we build, test, and prove our endurance and perseverance. As with any journey, there are many different types of challenges we may face. There can be challenges with the vehicle of transportation, the directions, the road traveled, or the environment.

Vehicle
When reflecting, examining, and assessing the vehicle in which you are

traveling, there are two questions to explore.
1. What is carrying you?
2. What are you carrying?

For the first question, to determine what is carrying you, examine the mindset, skillset, and toolset that enabled you to arrive at your current destination. What are the character traits, principles, routines, and habits that helped you arrive at your current state, level, and position? Differentiate the aspects of your routines that are essential and fruitful versus those that are futile and ineffective.

In exploring this question, it is also important to examine the mindset you have to ensure you are prepared for the journey ahead. I have had the experience of driving down the road and having something hit and crack my windshield. If left unaddressed, the crack grows wider and wider. The more space covered by the crack, the less visibility I had. In life, we can have previous situations or challenges that have left us with mental and emotional scars. If we do not immediately address those scars, they will grow to the point that they impact your vision and clarity when trying to look ahead.

Additionally, we need to regularly assess the mental and emotional signals we are exhibiting. If there is an issue with the vehicle's systems that prevents it from functioning as intended, a "check engine" light appears. The purpose of this light is to alert drivers that there is a problem that needs to be addressed, and until it is addressed, there may be functionality that is unavailable or will not work properly. Similarly, if we notice that our emotions are not balanced, or our tolerance level is depleted, we need to reflect, examine, and assess our mental and emotional state. If we notice that our instinctive actions and responses are not what they usually are, we again need to reflect, examine, and assess our mental and emotional state. Emotional responses, whether internally or externally exhibited, are not to be ignored. These are signals for an underlying issue that, if not addressed, may hinder your progression.

For the second question, to identify what you are carrying, examine what you are taking with you on your journey. You have arrived in the present from the journey of your past. It is time to unpack your baggage, throw away the trash, and store your souvenirs. What are the things you learned from your past experiences that you need to keep, and what are the things you need to let go?

A weigh station is a roadside checkpoint designed to assess the weight of vehicles traveling on the road. These weigh stations are important to ensure that vehicles stay within the weight limits that the various roadways can safely handle. Vehicles carrying loads over the regulated limits can damage the road for other drivers.

Achieve Your Purposed Potential

It is also important for us to regularly assess what we are carrying to ensure we have not picked up additional weights, burdens, or problems that we were not meant to carry. This ties to our earlier topic on the evolution of purpose: the difference between being capable and being called. Just because you think you are capable of carrying a load does not mean that you are called to carry that load during this leg of the journey. It may not be yours to carry. You may hinder someone else's growth or strengthening, while also weighing yourself down unnecessarily. We have to separate the call to serve from the avoidable weight of someone else's load when they are fully capable, equipped, and positioned to carry it themselves. Carrying additional loads will hinder our journey and cause damage.

Although we determined what we were taking with us at the beginning of the journey, at times we may pick up additional baggage along the way. Furthermore, we may find that we intended to leave something at our prior destination. But we may find that somehow it was not left behind and has accompanied us on our journey. Whether inadvertently carried or picked up along the way, this additional baggage constitutes extra weight that makes our journey more challenging.

We have the power to choose what we receive and keep from our experiences. Boats do not sink until the water on the outside of the boat gets on the inside of the boat. We choose what we allow in the boat that we are sailing in from shore to shore. When you go through an experience, are you bringing tools or lessons that will help you on your journey? Or are you bringing in negative perceptions, biases, or defeating thoughts that will sink you? By taking an active role in the maintenance and management of our mental processes and thoughts, we can purposefully and effectively design the structure by which we experience and interpret life.

It is not only the additional weight and baggage that we need to be aware of that we are carrying; we also must assess the message we are carrying during this leg of the journey. Consider these questions when identifying your message and contribution:

1. What have you gained from your past?
2. What have you learned from your journey that you can share with others?
3. What is the message that you are carrying to deliver to those you encounter during this leg of your transportation of transformation?

You have something to offer, something to contribute, and something to teach others in each leg of your transformative journey. Do not lose sight of the gifts you are carrying.

Directions

Issues related to the directions we are following can be categorized into two areas:

1. Clarity
2. Control

To see our directions clearly, we must emerge from the shadow of trauma, grief, and pain. We must see beyond the clouds of disappointment and hopelessness. Once we are able to see beyond these things, clarity is achieved. It is important to note that looking beyond the pain is not easy. Seeing through the pain is not automatic. The etymology of the word perspective is the compilation of two Latin verbs[35]. The first is perspicere, that means through. The second Latin root is specere, a verb that means to look. Therefore, the perspective we choose is a reflection of what we see beyond the current situation. To maintain clarity, we have to see beyond the obstacles and challenges. Seeing beyond and through obstacles and challenges requires us to choose the appropriate perspectives on our situation. As mentioned earlier, this may require the insights of others that you trust to provide the truth. This may require the activation of your corner or your personal advisory board.

Challenges do not come to stay. They come to pass. Since the challenges and storms we face are temporary, the storms should not be the focus. Your focus should be on what will remain after the storm has passed: your mind, body, emotions, and spirit. Those things that will remain after the storm passes must be protected.

When we reside in a stormy period of life for a long time. This stormy period may have been one wherein we were in a state of consistent crisis. We may have experienced trauma. We may have experienced marginalization. We may have experienced abuse or neglect. We may have experienced loss or rejection. While existing in these extended storms, we often develop a certain mindset to survive that storm. However, aspects of that mentality may hinder the development of the mindset you need to reach your purposed potential.

One aspect of the survival mentality that can hinder progress is indifference. There is trauma in trying when trying is not fruitful. The trauma that results from unfruitful efforts can be paralyzing. It can result in a state of apathy towards the future. When this mentality sets in, it impedes the transportation of transformation. The safety of the current comfort zone deceptively outweighs the risk of trying to transport to a new horizon. People can then make the decision not to climb due to the risk of injury from a potential fall. By not climbing, we settle for less than our purposed potential. Settling is the decision to accept less than what is justly due. To achieve our purposed potential, we cannot settle for less than we deserve. We deserve to achieve our purposed potential.

Another hindering mentality is that of hopelessness. This mentality leads people to adopt a fixed mindset, giving up hope for a transformed future. This begins with negative thinking, progresses to negative speech, and results in negative actions. A person with this mentality resembles the Winne the Pooh character, Eeyore. Eeyore is a pessimist. Eeyore consistently sees the negative side of every situation. Light escapes him. He attracts darkness. Similarly, when residing in the dark for so long, darkness becomes normal. People in a state of hopelessness will stop searching for light.

A third limiting mentality is fear. Pain can produce fear, hesitation, and paranoia. Even when the pain has passed, often fear can be part of the debris that is left from the storm. This

Achieve Your Purposed Potential

debris can hinder the rebuilding and renovation processes. It can hinder us from moving forward in a wiser, stronger, and better manner. It can cause us to live life avoiding pain instead of living life pursuing purpose. We can find ourselves going through life trying to not lose versus living life purposefully pursuing victory. Traveling through life with our foot on the brake will keep us from achieving our purposed potential.

To combat these mentality components, which can limit our clarity, we must ensure we choose a healthy perspective of our storms. This will allow us to ensure we are spending our time, energy, and focus on purposeful thoughts and actions. It is easy for our view to become cluttered by darkness and distractions. Therefore, we must take an active and aggressive role in protecting our mind, body, emotions, and spirit.

Achieve Your Purposed Potential

A perspective that was shared during a session in the Dharius Daniels transformational certification programs is that dark moments are actually dark rooms. This perspective struck a chord with me as I recall taking a photography course in seventh grade. In that course, I learned that photographers enter dark rooms with negatives. But if the negatives are processed correctly, the photographer will come out of that dark room with a clear picture. How are you processing your negative thoughts and emotions? It is through the effective processing of dark moments that the picture is made clear. In dark moments, the tools of focus and reframing are helpful to ensure effective processing.

As Albert Einstein once stated, "Adversity introduces a man to himself." It is what we do in the darkness that will reveal where we are developmentally. When things are unclear, we must slow down. Speed in darkness will result in injury. Therefore,

Achieve Your Purposed Potential

if we are in an unclear state, it is a time for reflection and preparation.

Reflect on your current position and ensure you are maximizing what you are receiving and giving in your current state. We can also use these time periods where clarity is lacking to prepare for the next leg of our journey. Reflection and preparation are helpful in safeguarding our mindset against darkness and distractions.

You may not always choose the storms that arise in your life. Some storms are not forecasted. But you can choose the impact you allow the storm to have. Not all storms come to disrupt and destroy your life; some storms actually come to clear your path. Use the storm to clear your path. Do not let it crush your plan. Use the storm to build you up. Do not let it break you. Use the storm to strengthen you. Do not let it shatter you.

Achieve Your Purposed Potential

We must also maintain control over the direction in which we are traveling. As we reflect on our life's journey, we may pinpoint portions of our lives where we have allowed ourselves to be moved from the driver seat of the vehicle. We have allowed other people to take the wheel, determining the direction we are traveling in our lives. We may have allowed past pain and trauma to take the wheel. We may have allowed fear or doubt to take the wheel and determine the direction we are traveling.

We must hold ourselves accountable for the choices we make in our lives, which determine the direction we travel. Even when limited options are presented to us, we are accountable for our decisions. This means that we may have to research and seek additional options than the ones that are brought to us. The songwriter Shawn Carter, more widely known as Jay-Z, articulated this accountability when he said, "Just know I chose my own fate. I drove by the fork in the road and went straight." The steps we take in life are marked by the choices we make. Each step is a choice. We are accountable for the choices we make and the direction we take.

Our direction also needs to be informed by current information. When the direction we take in life is influenced by historical information instead of current information, it can lead to incorrect choices. When driving to a destination, if we rely on outdated information for directions, changes and improvements that have been made will not be incorporated. Detours may now exist that did not previously exist. Traffic patterns may have changed. Traffic signs and lights may have been added. It is important to determine direction based on current information.

If our past becomes our compass, we will be misled. Fears and biases formed from your past should not be the primary basis for decisions in your direction. We have to take our current state, present power, and purposed potential into account to determine the direction we take in the transportation of transformation.

Road Traveled
The road we are traveling can also present challenges we must overcome during our transportation of transformation. It is important to pay attention when traveling down the path. There may be issues on the road, or there may be signs that will let us know what challenges may be ahead of us.

The road itself can contain challenging obstacles such as potholes or dangerous debris. A pothole is a pit that is formed in a road due to erosion caused by excessive use, weight, and exposure to environmental factors[37]. The path we take during our transportation of transformation may be worn out. We may deal with people who have the fixed mindset of expecting what has always been. Just because a path has been traveled by many does not mean that you cannot make it your own. As we apply our own gifts and talents, we can create new trails and give people around us new visions of what is possible.

It is also important to realize that the people we may encounter, the resources we may access, and the tools we may try to employ may pose challenges and obstacles. If we are not careful and intentional, these challenges and obstacles can be a distraction. The key is to maintain our focus on our development and our transformative process.

Debris
Some storms can leave debris behind. Debris refers to the scattered pieces that remain after a destructive event. To maintain our ability to endure and persevere, we must take inventory as we overcome challenges. If we are not careful, as we endure and overcome difficulties, we can be left exhausted

and weak. This exhaustion and weakness can result in the debris of doubt and fragility. To protect against debris that can trip us up, we must take the time to reflect, examine, and assess ourselves regularly. This will enable us to identify the areas we need to address.

We cannot pour from an empty cup. More importantly, we cannot pour from a broken cup. Therefore, it is important that we identify where we need to be refilled. We must then address those areas. This will enable us to endure, because our cups will not be broken and can hold our joy, hopes, and dreams. This will also enable us to persevere, as we will be able to pour all along the way.

Signs

As we continuously reflect, examine, and assess, we must identify the signs that are presented to us along the journey. At times, we may be presented with signs

signifying that a merging lane is ahead. This sign indicates that two paths are approaching a point where they will merge. There are many examples of situations in life that can signify that there is oncoming traffic. Expansion in your realm of responsibility or influence would indicate that you will have additional personalities, influences, and opinions that will enter your lane. In these situations, we must ensure that we do not lose ourselves, our identity, our focus, or our destination when merged with other traffic.

Another sign that may appear on the journey is a "Do Not Enter" sign. This sign alerts travelers that there are dangers beyond a particular point. It may be that the road is under construction or that beyond that point, travel is not possible or safe. This sign may materialize as trusted advice, a gut feeling, or an intuition that something may not be right. This sign may be an outcome of your reflection,

examination, and assessment. If the fruit of your journey is not in line with what you are seeking, then you may be traveling in the wrong direction. While traveling by means of the transportation of transformation, you should take inventory of your fruit (results) frequently. What results are you obtaining from your efforts? This assessment will help to ensure you are traveling in the correct direction to reach your desired destination.

When encountering signs indicating you are traveling in the wrong direction, a detour may be necessary. Taking a detour does not change your destination. It may change the time it takes to arrive at the destination, but that does not mean that the destination is unattainable. Detours require determination, commitment, perseverance, and patience. During the transportation of transformation, detour signs may appear as rejection, uneasiness, or unfruitful efforts. But as stated, these moments are actually moments of redirection. That one specific door may not have opened. But not all doors are for you. Some doors are trap doors. Ignoring a "Do Not Enter" sign and going through a trap door can lead to a position with no growth. It may leave you feeling stuck or stifled. Therefore, when we notice signs that we should not enter, we can redirect our efforts to a more fruitful path.

Our lives, at times, can take unexpected twists and turns. These unforeseen challenges can also cause us to take a detour from our intended path. Some of these twists and turns may be a loss, an unexpected change, a diagnosis, or devastating pain. In these cases, monitoring our mental and emotional state is paramount. It is critical to give ourselves grace as we process through these types of changes. The detour we

Achieve Your Purposed Potential

take in these moments is a path of its own. There is no timetable for the detour of overcoming pain. As stated earlier, the detour does not keep us from reaching the destination. It is important that we take the time we need to cope and persevere.

Another sign that you may encounter during the transportation of  transformation is the u-turn sign. Once the signs that we are traveling in the wrong direction appear, we will need to perform a u-turn to reverse our direction. As previously mentioned, the longer we wait to turn around, the longer it will take to reach our desired destination.

Making a u-turn and changing directions takes strength, courage, and vulnerability. At times, we may have to acknowledge that we have made errors, mistakes, and incorrect decisions. By acknowledging these things that may have caused a wrong direction, we are teaching those that are around us. We are teaching them that we all make mistakes. We are teaching them that it is good to acknowledge when you have made a wrong decision. We are teaching them that when we acknowledge that things are going wrong, we do not have to continue to go down the wrong path. We are demonstrating for them the strength, vision, humility, grit, and grace required to make necessary u-turns in life.

Environment
There are also environmental factors to prepare for in order to persevere during the transportation of transformation. One environmental factor is the season. There is a story that depicts an important point regarding seasons[36]. There was once a man with four sons. He wanted his sons to learn about the seasons of life. The father sent each of his sons on a mission to observe a pear tree that was far away. The first son took his journey in the winter. The

second went to observe the tree in the spring. The third son embarked on the mission in the summer. The youngest son went in the fall. When they had all completed their journeys, they gathered together. He asked each son to describe what they had seen so that they could determine what to do about the tree.

The first son, who saw the tree in the winter, said that the tree should be destroyed. He said the tree was dry, ugly, and twisted. The second son, who saw the tree in the spring, said they should be patient. He said the tree was covered with buds and had much potential and promise. The third son saw things differently. He saw the tree in the summer. He said the tree provided a perfect view. He said the tree was beautiful and full of blossoms that smelled amazing. The last son saw the tree in the fall. He said the tree was very fruitful and productive. It was ripe and full of fruit. He thought they could sell the fruit and generate revenue. The man then explained to his sons that they were all correct.

The father further explained that each of them had only seen the tree in one season of the tree's life. The lesson in this story is that you cannot judge a tree, or a person, place, or thing, by only one season. If you pass judgment based on a difficult season, you will miss the promise, beauty, and fulfillment of all other seasons.

Do not judge yourself by one difficult season. Do not let the pain of one season rob you of the beauty that exists within future seasons. If we define ourselves by the way we appear in the winter season, we will allow people to treat us as an ugly, dry, and twisted tree. We may allow people to cut us down and tear us apart. We may feel we don't deserve a spot in a beautiful space. We may feel we have nothing to offer others. We will act ugly, dry, and twisted, because that is how we see ourselves. However, if we hold on to

Achieve Your Purposed Potential

our belief in our purposed potential, we will understand that we are in the middle of our transformation. We will not limit ourselves to one season. We will not cut ourselves or others down because we know we simply need time to bear fruit. No matter how dark or hard it is, a new season is coming. A season of fruit-bearing is on the way.

Another aspect of seasons that is important to be aware of is the purpose of the season. Each season has a preparation, a purpose, and a product. The winter season provides a cleansing and purifying process that prepares the plants for the spring. The product of the winter is that with all the buds, flowers, and fruit falling from the tree, you can see the core. When difficulty hits, it can clarify things. It can simplify things. It can show you who your true friends are and who your true family is. In the winter season, you will learn the areas that you need to work on that were hidden by the successes you had and the fruit you yielded. When the cheers and accolades are stripped away, what is left? What is at your core? What is left to motivate you and push you forward? The winter season will identify these things.

The spring season prepares the tree for the summer. In this season, the seed begins to take root and starts to bud. Spring is the season of budding and of new beginnings. In this season, you learn the depth of your willingness to plant seeds. You will test your willingness to give your time, energy, effort, gifts, and talents towards a harvest that will come in a future season. The start, the first steps, and the emergence are necessary for the full bloom that will come in the summer.

The summer is the season of blooming. This is the season where you begin to see the blooms of your start. In the summer, the blooms smell amazing and look beautiful. The work you have begun starts to take shape. It is preparation for the fall season, when the fruit of the work emerges. In the summer season, you learn the possibilities of your seed and work.

The fall season is the season of harvest. This is when the work transitions from being beautiful to view and delightful to smell to being fruitful. This is when the substance of the work is made evident. It is nourishing and sustaining. But it takes work to reap a harvest. In this season, you learn the effectiveness of the seed and work you put in during the earlier seasons. Each season has a purpose. It is important to take notice of what you are learning about yourself in each season.

It is also important to be aware of the weather. The weather represents the condition of the atmosphere in the space you occupy. The atmosphere is denoted by the people, places, or things around you. Depending on the atmosphere you are in, adjustments may need to be made. Some storms and some shifts in the atmosphere are forecasted. We have to prepare for the forecast. But we cannot get so attached to the forecast that we ignore reality. We have to have and employ the necessary tools to adapt to reality when it is different from what we expected. Are there attitudes, biases, or characteristics that require an adjustment to ensure the desired outcomes are reached in a manner that is safe and fruitful?

As an example, one painful yet critical lesson that I have learned in life is that not all environments you will travel through will welcome your transformation. There are some people and places that would prefer you stay in your limited state. Some would prefer that you stay in a place without purpose or clarity.

In these environments, it does not mean you need to stop progressing. In these instances, you simply have to adjust your wardrobe to match the weather. Practically, it means that in these environments, you would need to be careful what and how much you share. In these environments, move in silence. Continue to gain new mindsets, toolsets, and skillsets, progressing in your journey of transformation. But if communicating your goals and progress in that environment is not safe or would cause repercussions, you do not have to communicate your progress. This is similar to laying a foundation. If you are in an environment where people are stomping and trampling over each other, you may want to lay the concrete and protect it until it dries. This way, it can dry completely before the footsteps are imprinted upon it in a manner that would hold the footprints forever.

Additionally, another component of our environment is the people around us. One lesson in this area is to not compare yourself to other travelers. Your starting point and your destination are different from those of every other driver. Focus on your development and progression. Strive to be better today than you were yesterday.

Another lesson is to observe the fruit of your relationships. Nurture your relationships to maximize the fruit that is obtained. Once we identify what we need within the current season, we must communicate and act within that understanding. This may entail gaining new relationships, changing the nature of relationships, or creating necessary boundaries. We cannot assume that others around us know who we truly are, where we are headed, and what we need to get there.

At one point in my life, I was in a winter season. Things were challenging, confusing, and hard. I had advisors who saw the battles I was fighting, and they attempted to throw in the towel for me. However, I was in a position to catch the towel before it hit the mat and declare, "I am not done fighting!"

Achieve Your Purposed Potential

In all these things, whether issues arise related to the vehicle, directions, the road traveled, the signs we encounter, or the environment around you, there must be a mindset of determination to enable you to persevere.

There is a song titled "The Square Root of Possible". In this song, the ability to transcend boundaries and limitations is raised. The chorus of the song states, "Watch me rise high above my obstacles. Watch me become who I'm supposed to be." In these lines, the songwriter, Madalen Mills, is expressing that obstacles are not a stopping point. It is possible to overcome obstacles. To overcome obstacles, a mindset of determination is necessary. Through transformation, we can be transported above our obstacles and beyond our perceived limitations.

In the bridge of this song, it states, "Shut the windows and lock the doors. I'll take the roof off, and then I'll soar." This is where the determined mindset is truly shown. These words carry life-changing power, particularly for anyone who has faced closed windows and locked doors. I love the boldness, the audacity, and the grit in these words. This is not a wishful expression; it is a bold declaration! To achieve our purpose and goals in life and to reach our destination of purposed potential, we must have this level of grit, determination, and perseverance to refuse to give in when it gets tough or when the destination seems far away.

We may face closed windows and locked doors. But we have to be determined that those limitations and obstacles will not stop us. We will persevere to reach our purposed potential. We do not need a door! We do not need a window! We can blow the roof off because our purpose and our vision cannot be confined to a building. We will find a way, or create a way. But we will not stop pursuing our purposed potential. Therefore, we must identify any limitations, obstacles, or excuses we are operating within. The destruction of these barriers is necessary for us to complete our transformative journey.

The Destination Becomes the Starting Point

We must continuously grow, develop, and transform. There is a saying that conveys, "There are places a butterfly can go that a caterpillar cannot." This was a saying I heard when I was a child. I developed a love for butterflies and the power of transformation. However, I later learned that once a caterpillar transforms into a butterfly, it only lives for a few weeks. This then made me question the use of the butterfly as an example of the power of transformation. But I came to realize that this shortened life expectancy still raises an important lesson in the true power of transformation.

The reason that a caterpillar dies shortly after it transforms into a butterfly is because it stops transforming. Once it becomes a butterfly, there are external factors that the previous transformation did not sufficiently overcome. Therefore, additional transformation would be necessary for the butterfly to survive and thrive. Transformation must be a continuous process. The new destination reached becomes the starting point. It is the launching point for the next leg of the journey of transformation. We must continuously reflect, examine, and assess to persistently improve.

Continuous assessment and improvement of the mindset, skillset, and toolset are necessary. We have to continue to monitor and adjust our mindset as necessary to ensure that we optimize our skillset and toolset along our journey of transformation. Kaizen is a model of continuous improvement introduced by Masaaki Imai[12]. The word Kaizen means improvement. Although it is often applied within the context of the professional work environment, the impact of continuous improvement is not confined to one area of life. Within this model, key areas are identified, assessed, and improved in a continuous manner. It is an effective model to apply to the ongoing process of continuously assessing and improving your mindset, skillset, and toolset. One process that is helpful in achieving the continuous improvement goals of Kaizen is a series of steps represented by the acronym PDCA[13]:

- Plan
- Do
- Check
- Act

During the planning step, a goal is defined and a path to reach the goal is outlined. It is critical to have clarity about the goal and the vision of what success looks like. This vision of success is what will be used in the check phase. What is the objective you wish to reach during this cycle or journey of improvement? The do step is where the plan is executed. It is helpful in this phase to have mitigation plans in case challenges and complications occur. It is much easier to establish mitigation plans prior to experiencing issues than when the pressure of the situation is heightened. The check step ensures results are aligned with the defined goals and objectives. Are the key results expected to be achieved? If not, adjustments would need to be made to ensure the goal is reached. The act step includes sustaining activities, resetting standards, and defining the next level of improvement.

With each level of growth achieved, standards should be reassessed. The standards I had a decade ago should not be the same standards I am operating with today. I have grown since then, so I am not willing to go back to where I was ten years ago from a mindset, skillset, or toolset perspective. As Oliver Wendell Holmes stated, "A man's mind is stretched by a new idea or sensation and never shrinks back to its former dimensions." We must be good stewards of our growth and development. Growth is not easy. Our growth needs to mean something. Therefore, we should reestablish our standards to reflect the value we place on our growth and development.

The diagram below depicts this evolutionary process of growth and development. Your transportation from level to level of growth and development is achieved through the transformation earned through a process of developing your mindset, skillset, and toolset. The process of development includes the four steps of plan, do, check, and act. At each level, a new standard is defined, and a targeted growth level is set.

Achieve Your Purposed Potential

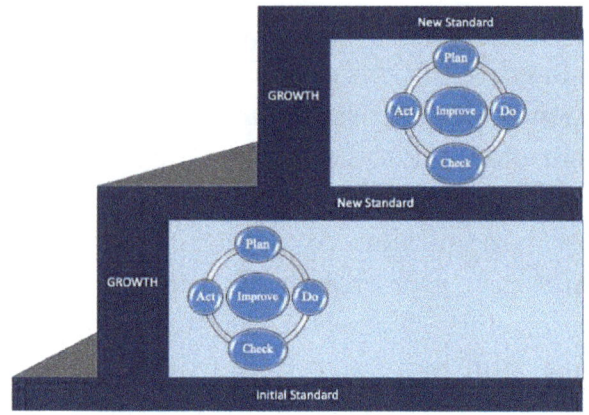

This process of continuous learning, growth, development, and transformation provides exponential returns on the investment of time, energy, focus, and effort. Principally, when we are intentional about our goals for growth and transformation, we can architect our path to our purposed potential.

The purposed potential is the next destination of the journey. But the journey is never-ending. We do not stop growing. We do not stop developing. We do not stop transforming. Our environment and

Achieve Your Purposed Potential

the world around us are constantly changing. We therefore need to have something to set our focus on so that we do not get lost in the winds and waves of change. Our focus, purpose, and direction are what keep us from floating aimlessly.

As we reach each destination of transformative growth, we should take a moment to celebrate our progress. Every step forward is a step to be celebrated. It is also important to note that forward can be defined in many ways. It is important to define forward based on the season in which you are currently operating. Forward may be developing mentally, emotionally, or spiritually. Striving for the next level of development is a definition of moving forward. In some seasons, forward may be defined as finding the strength to stand and show up. Finding the hope, courage, and determination to try again can be another definition of moving forward. As Dr. Martin Luther King Jr. inspired us, "If you can't fly, then run.

Achieve Your Purposed Potential

If you can't run, then walk. If you can't walk, then crawl. But whatever you do, you have to keep moving forward."

Leverage the key principles we covered to continuously transform. The following principles will prepare you and sustain you along each leg of the journey:

1. Power & Strength
2. Speed & Momentum
3. Balance & Flexibility
4. Endurance & Perseverance

We cannot settle for the destination we have reached. There is another level of purposed potential for which we can strive and achieve. Why settle for small tweaks and small improvements when transformative growth and unprecedented progress are possible? Settling is easy. But easy is not fulfilling. Easy is not your purposed potential. This applies regardless of outward success. You can be the best in your field, class, or area of focus. But if it is

Achieve Your Purposed Potential

not *your* best, then it is not enough. If it is not *your* purposed potential, then there is more progress to be made and a greater destination of progress to reach.

As the quotation introduced by John Shedd states, "A ship in harbor is safe, but that is not what ships are built for."[20] When you are not actively preparing for and moving towards what you are built for, you will experience internal conflict and frustration. Do not settle for less than what you deserve. You deserve your best. You deserve the fruit that comes from achieving the next level of purposed potential.

Another cause of settling that exists is fatigue. This is why endurance and perseverance is so critical. Some legs of the transportation of transformation can seem immensely long and laboriously hard. Focusing on what will come as a result of your endurance and perseverance will help to provide energy in those moments when fatigue creeps in. Leveraging the tools and activities you identified that provide you with energy and joy will also help in these moments of fatigue. Whatever you do, do not give up and do not settle.

When we are unaware of the value we hold within our presence, time, energy, and effort, we will settle for and tolerate less than what we deserve. Therefore, I will end this book the way it began: **You have value.**

Leverage the value within you to gain more growth and to leverage the transportation of transformation to achieve your wildest dreams.

You deserve to reach your dreams.

Resources

1. https://plato.stanford.edu/entries/authenticity/#:~:text=The%20term%20'authentic'%20is%20used,"reliable%2C%20accurate%20representation".

2. https://psychology.iresearchnet.com/social-psychology/control/authenticity/#:~:text=From%20this%20perspective%2C%20the%20essence,and%20(4)%20relational%20orientation.

3. https://depts.washington.edu/matseed/batteries/MSE/battery.html#:~:text=A%20battery%20is%20a%20device,%2Dreduction%20(redox)%20reaction.

4. https://www.ncpedia.org/motto-esse-quam-videri-be-rather

5. https://www.thechinastory.org/yearbooks/yearbook-2020-crisis/forum-standing-on-a-precipice/the-etymology-of-the-character-wei-%E5%8D%B1/

6. Welch, M. (1921). The Touch of The Master's Hand.

7. https://byjus.com/commerce/difference-between-financial-leverage-and-operating-leverage/#:~:text=There%20are%20thre

e%20proportions%20of,the%20impact%20of%20fixed%20cost.

8. https://www.physicsclassroom.com/class/newtlaws/Lesson-1/Newton-s-First-Law

9. https://www1.grc.nasa.gov/beginners-guide-to-aeronautics/newtons-laws-of-motion/#:~:text=Newton's%20Second%20Law%3A%20Force&text=His%20second%20law%20defines%20a,object%20times%20its%20velocity%20V.

10. https://www.worldbank.org/en/topic/skillsdevelopment

11. https://www.linkedin.com/pulse/14-law-skill-building-best-metaphor-development-skillset-kearns/

12. Kaizen: The Key To Japan's Competitive Success; Publisher : McGraw-Hill Education; 1st edition (November 1, 1986); Masaaki Imai

13. https://www.mindtools.com/as2l5i1/pdca-plan-do-check-act

14. https://w5coaching.com/key-concepts-2/

15. Duhigg, C. (2013). *The power of habit.* Random House Books.

16. Clear, J. (2018). *Atomic habits: tiny changes, remarkable results : an easy & proven way to build good habits & break bad ones.* New York, Avery, an imprint of Penguin Random House.

17. Rubin, G. (2015). *Better than before: What I learned About Making and Breaking Habits--to Sleep More, Quit Sugar, Procrastinate Less, and Generally Build a Happier Life.* Crown.

18. Hutchinson, A. (2021). *Endure: Mind, body, and the curiously elastic limits of human performance.* Custom House.

19. Noakes TD. The central governor model of exercise regulation applied to the marathon. Sports Med. 2007;37(4-5):374-7. doi: 10.2165/00007256-200737040-00026. PMID: 17465612.

20. Shedd, John (1928). *Salt from my attic.* The Mosher Press, Portland, Maine. Nearsighted vs. Farsighted: What's the Difference? June 1, 2022.

21. https://www.healthline.com/health/nearsighted-vs-farsighted#farsightedness

22. West, T. G., West, G. S., Plato, & Aristophanes. (1998). *Four texts on Socrates: Plato's Euthyphro, Apology, and Crito, and Aristophanes' Clouds* (Rev. ed.). Cornell University Press.

23. Square Root of Possible by Madalen Mills; Release Date: November 13, 2020

24. https://www.cnn.com/2008/US/09/18/ike.last.house.standing/

25. https://omegadrivingschool.com/driver-blind-spots-what-they-are-and-how-to-reduce-them/

26. https://www.verywellmind.com/cognitive-biases-distort-thinking-2794763

27. https://www.yalemedicine.org/news/covid-timeline

28. Justice League Unlimited: https://www.imdb.com/title/tt0766996/characters/nm0627624

29. https://purposefocuscommitment.com/funny-story-using-tools-right-way/?_page=2

30. Bush, R. (2021). *Designing the Mind: The principles of psychitecture.*

31. https://www.ourendangeredworld.com/are-lions-the-king-of-the-jungle/

32. https://www.palauosp.org/2020/02/20/osp-hosts-ussecretservice-counterfeit-currency-training/

33. https://www.ncbi.nlm.nih.gov/books/NBK557811/

34. https://www.helpguide.org/articles/mental-health/emotional-intelligence-eq.htm

35. https://www.etymonline.com/word/perspective

36. https://medium.com/the-mission/the-four-seasons-of-us-47238538149

37. https://mtc.ca.gov/sites/default/files/APWA_Pothole_Fact_Sheet.pdf

38. https://www.independent.co.uk/news/science/duck-and-rabbit-illusion-b1821663.html

39. https://www.livescience.com/63645-optical-illusion-young-old-woman.html